THE SEARCH FOR PEACE

The Rt Hon. Lord Hurd of Westwell, CH, CBE enjoyed a distinguished career in government spanning sixteen years. He was educated at Eton and Trinity College, Cambridge, where he obtained a first-class degree in history and was President of the Cambridge Union. After joining the Diplomatic Service, he went on to serve at the Foreign Office in Peking, New York and Rome. He ran Edward Heath's private office from 1968 to 1970 and acted as his Political Secretary at 10 Downing Street from 1970 to 1974.

Following terms as Minister of State in the Foreign Office and the Home Office, he became Secretary of State for Northern Ireland (1984–85) and Home Secretary (1985–89) before his appointment as Foreign Secretary in 1989. He was MP for Mid-Oxfordshire (later Witney) from 1974 until 1997.

Upon his retirement as Foreign Secretary in 1995, Lord Hurd was appointed Deputy Chairman of NatWest Markets and a main board director of the NatWest Group. In 1998 he became Deputy Chairman of Coutts & Co. and Chairman of the Advisory Committee of Hawkpoint Partners Limited, the corporate advisory partnership owned by NatWest. He is also Deputy Chairman of British Invisibles and Chairman of the Prison Reform Trust charity.

Douglas Hurd, who is the author of ten books, lives in Oxfordshire with his wife Judy and their son and daughter. He has three grown-up sons from his first marriage.

THE
SEARCH
FOR
PEACE

DOUGLAS
HURD

WARNER BOOKS

A *Warner* Book

First published in Great Britain in 1997
by Little, Brown and Company

A CIP catalogue record for this book is
available from the British Library

ISBN 0 7515 2673 8

Typeset in Bembo by Solidus (Bristol) Ltd
Printed and bound in Great Britain by
Clays Ltd, St. Ives plc

Warner Books
A Division of Little, Brown and Company (UK)
Brettenham House
Lancaster Place
London WC2E 7EN

To Judy

CONTENTS

ACKNOWLEDGEMENTS

This book accompanies a television series made with the BBC. I am grateful to them, and in particular to Matthew Barrett, the producer, for his artistry and wisdom. Many of the ideas in the book come from my conversations with those I interviewed for the series: Kofi Annan, Lucius Battle, Boutros Boutros Ghali, Robert Bowie, Rolf Ekeus, Valery Giscard d'Estaing, Lord Healey, Henry Kissinger, General Jacques Paul Klein, Robert McNamara, Sodana Ogata, Sir Frank Roberts, Helmut Schmidt, Arthur Schlesinger Jr, President Eduard Shevardnadze, Javior Solana.

But a book can carry much more thought than a television series. This is not a book of memoirs; the time for that has not yet come. But I have tried to distil here as many of the impressions and conclusions of my working life as are relevant to the chosen theme. This is thus a personal book of which I have drafted every word myself. But it owes much to talk with friends and former colleagues – too many, in fact, to list. For example, Professor David Dilks, Vice-Chancellor of Hull University, and Sir John Weston, our Ambassador at the UN, provided clues which would otherwise have escaped me. My former Private Secretary John Sawers has been generous with ideas and comments. Julia Broad deciphered my scribbles and tapes with remarkable skill. Alan Samson and

Caroline North of Little, Brown were at hand to answer cries for help. But any foolishness and any omissions in the book are mine. I have thoroughly enjoyed putting it together.

INTRODUCTION

Previous page *Arthur Balfour (Foreign Secretary 1916–1919), one of many half-believers, addresses the first meeting of the Council of the League of Nations.*
The Hulton Getty Picture Collection Limited

W e live in a world of nation states which are both immortal and incompetent.

They are immortal because most of them continue to act as a focus for the loyalty of the citizen. That is not to say that they remain unchanged. The twentieth century has seen many such changes, but through fission rather than fusion. The colonial empires have dissolved into nation states; so has the Soviet Union. So have states like Czechoslovakia and Yugoslavia which were put together for reasons of diplomatic and economic convenience. In Western Europe a determined and idealistic attempt has been made to fuse nation states into a politically integrated unity, but to me at least this effort seems unlikely to reach that final objective, precisely because a sufficient number of the citizens of Europe continue to feel that their first loyalty is to their nation. Ask an Italian what he is, and he will still say an Italian.

Yet the nation states are also incompetent. Not one of them, not even the United States as the single remaining super-power, can adequately provide for the needs that its citizens now articulate. The extent of that incompetence has become sharply clearer during this century. The inadequacy of national govern-ments to provide security, prosperity or a decent environment has brought into being a huge array of international rules, con-ferences and institutions; the only answer to the puzzle of the immortal but incompetent nation state is effective co-operation between those states for all the purposes that lie beyond the reach of any one of them.

One inadequacy was clear long before the twentieth century. A Europe of nation states always signified a Europe of wars. There was no doubt about the evil consequences of war. Henry V, moving anonymously through his troops on the eve of Agincourt, captured the mixture of excitement and anxiety with which Shakespeare's generation contemplated war. But for most of them the solution was victory, and a peace which the victor imposed upon the vanquished.

This book, and the accompanying television series that I helped the BBC to produce, starts with the next stage, when it became clear that victory was not enough. In the early years of the nineteenth century the Allied powers had conquered the French Revolution and dethroned Napoleon. But gathering in Vienna in 1814 they recognised that they had been deeply frightened and scarred. Indeed their discussions about the nature of the new peace were interrupted by the return of Napoleon from Elba and the campaign at Waterloo. They won again, and this time the Emperor who had given them such a fright was finally removed to St Helena. But sober, intelligent men like Metternich, Castlereagh, and Talleyrand as representative of the defeated power, had learned from harsh experience that Europe needed a settlement that went some way beyond the redrawing of frontiers and the redistribution of colonies.

The settlement of Vienna was a conservative one. It aimed at a peace based upon settled frontiers and the acceptance of existing dynasties. Wisely it imposed no particular penalties on the defeated France, although the French had terrified the ruling classes of Europe, first with their Revolution and then with their Emperor. There was no recognition at Vienna that individuals should necessarily have a say in the choice of their own government, or indeed the choice of which country they lived in. Kings and emperors were back on their thrones; peoples had to forget the fall of the Bastille and learn again how to obey. Neither democracy nor nationalism held the field because both concepts had been used by the French to stir up trouble. Britain was made uneasy by the settlement and refused to take part in the machinery set up to enforce it. This was partly because Britain was reluctant to make promises about involvement in Europe, partly because the British had a vague feeling that it would be a mistake to support the rulers of Europe constantly without regard for the wishes of their subjects.

Despite British hesitations, the settlement of Vienna worked pretty well by European standards. It faltered during the Crimean War and during the Franco-Prussian War. It was complicated by the manoeuvres of Bismarck and dislocated by the much less skilful thrust of the Kaiser. The foundation of the European system also shifted through the decades. Having originally rested on a concert of powers acting together, it was eventually based on a balance of European alliances ranged against one another – Germany and Austria ranged against Russia and France, with Britain hovering indistinctly behind the French. The system was suddenly brought into peril in the summer of 1914 and its collapse was accompanied by a slaughter unmatched in previous European history.

I chose to begin *The Search for Peace* not with the Congress of Vienna, but with my uncle's grave on the Somme. I was given his Christian name. I have his cap badge and the fatal telegram handed to my grandmother in Highgate. All the Company Commanders of the Seventh Battalion of the Middlesex Regiment were killed on the same day in September 1916. They were volunteers, who chose to go to war because their country was in danger. It is still rightly called the Great War because no war before had left the same footprint on history. The civil societies that had gradually grown strong in each nation during the nineteenth century were strained to breaking point. They broke in Germany, Russia and the Austro-Hungarian Empire. They almost broke in Britain and France. The peoples of all countries came out of that war determined that it should not be repeated. The system of Vienna and the concept of the balance of power were discredited. Europe was open to a whirlwind from the West. The American President, Woodrow Wilson, took Europe by storm. He denounced the whole system of a balance of power, secret diplomacy and frontiers designed to suit dynasties rather than the wishes of people. He preached a doctrine of idealism. He argued that only a peace based on democracy and justice would endure.

During the negotiations for the Treaty of Versailles American idealism came into uncomfortable conflict with the realities of Europe. The British half believed in the doctrines of Woodrow Wilson, the French not at all. The resulting settlement pleased no one. The League of Nations was founded on high principles, but given no power to enforce them. The Americans, having preached their way into Europe, refused to take responsibility for the settlement that followed. The Germans were harshly punished and therefore resentful, but the French were given no effective guarantee against a German revival. The British were subject to a confused mix of emotions out of which a determination to avoid a future war emerged as the strongest. The poems of Wilfred Owen and Siegfried Sassoon did their work, as the war memorials were unveiled in every town and village. The Versailles Settlement was stronger in idealism but weaker in realism than the settlement at Vienna, and lasted twenty years instead of a hundred. Its pretensions were swept away by the clear-eyed brutality of Nazis and Fascists, while the equally clear-eyed Communists waited on the sidelines.

The wheel came round the third time in 1945. We were given yet another chance in the search for peace. This time there was less cloudy idealism, but for this a price was paid. There was not much moralising at Potsdam or Yalta. It had to be acknowledged that the Soviet Union as one of the victorious powers would only accept a peace which consolidated its own power in Central and Eastern Europe, and indeed in the new United Nations, to an extent which could not be justified on any grounds of principle. Moreover, the peace of 1945 increasingly rested on the threat of nuclear war and what was called mutually assured destruction. The realistic strand in American foreign policy, which had always been there since the days of the Monroe Doctrine, began to assert itself more stridently alongside the idealism and the generosity. If

Woodrow Wilson had been President of the United States in 1945, would he have agreed to drop the atomic bomb?

Yet the world which resulted from the settlement after Hiroshima was better founded than its predecessor after the Treaty of Versailles. In particular the United Nations, despite its history of occasional paralysis and of bloated institutions, is a more promising instrument than was ever the League of Nations.

The fourth turn of the wheel came in 1989 with the sudden collapse of Communism, accompanied by the dissolution of the Soviet Union. This time there was no victorious battle, no peace conference, no one moment when a new settlement emerged out of chaos. We are still devising the fourth chapter in the search for peace.

My time as Foreign Secretary began in 1989, close to the collapse of the Berlin Wall and ended in 1995 just before the Dayton Peace Agreement brought an end for the time being to the war in Bosnia. During the first part of this period the international news seemed almost uniformly good. Communism was destroyed by the citizens who had been subjected to it. The Soviet Union collapsed and with it the threat of nuclear war. Immediately afterwards a straightforward act of aggression in the Middle East was reversed by an imposing international coalition when Saddam Hussein was thrown out of Kuwait.

Later the news turned sour. Whether in Somalia or Rwanda, in Croatia or Bosnia, the world showed itself incapable of resolving civil wars. This was a new task for which the institutions of the UN, NATO and the European Union are not equipped. Yet suddenly it became a task which public opinion required of governments and international institutions, as the peculiar savagery of civil wars was transmitted through television into every living room. 'Something must be done' came the cry on each occasion; but it was a confused cry not linked with any particular willingness to risk lives or assume the thankless role of umpire or emperor.

If civil wars have recently filled the television screens, other dangers have not gone away. The United States will not for ever enjoy its present pre-eminence. The risk from some wayward aggressor with a nuclear weapon has if anything increased. We face terrorism, the drug trade, the overflow of religious and ethnic hatred into violence. History is certainly not dead.

George Bush was the best leader the West has known since Truman immediately after the last war. But when Bush spoke of a new world order he was describing something towards which he hoped to lead the United States and the rest of us rather than something which had already been achieved. So far we have neither thrown away our fourth chance nor made full use of it. The outcome is still in the balance. We certainly shall not make good use of the opportunity unless we understand the nature of the first three attempts and what we can learn from them. So what are the lessons? What are the prospects? The aim of this book is to find a thread through the labyrinth.

CHAPTER ONE

1814 – 1939

Previous page *British troops going over the top in the Battle of the Somme, July—November 1916. The Allies lost a million and a quarter men; the bodies of 70,000 were never recovered.*
Popperfoto

My grandparents lived in a small Georgian house on Jacksons Lane which runs steeply up from the Archway Road to the old village of Highgate in North London. As children we used to visit them often, for they were cheerful and hospitable. We got to know the house well and the sloping garden intersected with paths, ideal for treasure hunts and hide and seek. But there was one room, the largest in the house, which we never visited. The drawing room was on the first floor – elegant, scrupulously tidy, with a grand piano in the corner. I suppose it was quite normal in the 1930s that children should not frequent the drawing rooms of their grandparents. What struck us as strange even then was that our grandparents did not use the room either. It was a room not for the present but for the past. Although no one ever described it as such the drawing room was a shrine, dominated by photographs and medals.

At zero hour on 15 September 1916 a huge artillery barrage by British guns opened a fresh round of the offensive called the Battle of the Somme. At zero plus five D Company of the Seventh Battalion of the Middlesex Regiment went over the top, led by a twenty-one-year-old captain, Douglas Hurd.

A day or two later my grandparents received a telegram which was followed by a letter.

> *Dear Mr Hurd,*
>
> *It is with deepest regret that I have to inform you that your son was killed in the attack of the 15th. Our battalion was assaulting the hostile positions . . . when there were signs of a counter-attack to our right. He moved out his Lewis guns to meet it and whilst observing the results of their fire, was shot through the head. His end was absolutely painless . . . Not only have I lost in him a most valuable officer, but I have also lost a personal friend whose companionship was always a pleasure to me. I am sorry to say that on the 15th our battalion was met with that tragedy, which has befallen so many other battalions in this war, and that we have to deplore the loss of very many of our officers and men. I pray that you and your family will accept the deepest sympathy of myself, and of the few officers now left to me, in your deepest sorrow.*
>
> *Yours very sincerely, Colonel E. J. King*

The Colonel must have written many similar letters. All the other company commanders of his battalion were killed on that day. So was the Prime Minister's son, Raymond Asquith. A young officer named Harold Macmillan was badly wounded. It was a bad day: but there were no good days.

Eighteen months later my grandparents' second son Jack, serving with the Hertfordshire Regiment, was overwhelmed during the last great German offensive of the war eight months before it ended. He fell on ground which the Germans took and his body was never recovered.

My grandmother pasted that letter from the Colonel about Uncle Douglas into a black album, together with the first fatal telegram, the later telegram from the King and Queen and a multitude of condoling letters, some with black edges. The most moving of these were written with stubs of pencil from the trenches. When one considers what the NCOs and men of the Middlesex Regiment were going through as they wrote, there is something special about these stilted, careful letters of sympathy with their sloping old-fashioned script. The sergeant and the corporal found the time and imagination to put themselves for a moment in the place of my shattered grandparents in Highgate.

The story of the Great War is composed of millions of such episodes. The tale of slaughter has been told over and over again by historians, novelists and above all poets. It lasted four years and three months. On average 5,600 soldiers were killed on each of those days. On the first day of the Battle of the Somme 20,000 British soldiers were killed. The story never ceases to appal. It is summed up by an American in Scott Fitzgerald's novel *Tender is the Night*.

> *See that little stream – we could walk to it in two minutes. It took the British a month to walk to it – a whole Empire walking very slowly, dying in front and pushing forward behind. And another empire walked very slowly backward a few inches a day, leaving the dead like a million bloody rugs. No European will ever do that again in this generation.*

Because of the immensity of the slaughter and the suffering the character of the Great War changed as it proceeded. At the beginning it was a patriotic war as other wars had been. The crowds cheered, the volunteers poured in, young men falsified their dates of birth so that they could fight. For the British and French in particular the issues were straightforward. France had been attacked. The invasion of Belgium was not only wicked but an unmistakable threat to the security of Britain. But as the war dragged on and the killing increased it seemed no longer sufficient simply to win an orthodox war and achieve an ortho-dox peace, to be succeeded no doubt by another orthodox war a few years later. It seemed essential to put an end not just to the current war but to the whole system which made such wars possible.

The entry of the United States into the war in the spring of 1917 put its eventual outcome beyond doubt. But the same event catapulted the President of the United States to a position of unique authority in the world. Woodrow Wilson was chief missionary of the new order and entirely contemptuous of the old. His attempt at a new order was gallant, principled – and a failure. In his anxiety to sweep away the old order Woodrow Wilson failed to notice that it had foundations which his new structure never achieved. The story of the nineteenth century was not only one of clashing empires, immoral alliances and down-trodden peoples. If that had been all then the nations would not have been strong enough to make that huge doomed effort in the Great War. The American already quoted in *Tender is the Night* went on to explain how they did it:

> *This took religion and years of plenty and tremendous sureties and the exact relation that existed between the classes. The Russians and*

Italians weren't any good on this front. You had to have a whole souled sentimental equipment going back further than you could remember. You had to remember Christmas and postcards of the Crown Prince and his fiancee and little cafes in Valence and beer gardens in Under den Linden and weddings at the Mairie and going to the Derby and your grandfather's whiskers . . . this kind of battle was invented by Lewis Carroll and Jules Verne and whoever wrote Undine and country deacons bowling and Marraines in Marseilles and girls seduced in the back lanes of Wurtemberg and Westphalia. Why this was a love battle – there was a century of middle-class love spent here. This was the last love battle.

It was the achievement of the nineteenth century to create these solid nation-based civilisations which in the West survived, however mauled, the awfulness of the Great War. Woodrow Wilson and those who joined him in making the peace settlement after that war were not wrong to attempt something new and definitive. But they might have fared better had they looked back to the settlement after the last great conflict – the settlement that, despite occasional breakdowns and obvious defects, had made possible the rooting of these substantial societies in a century of rapid transformation. The nineteenth century, like the twentieth, was a period of extraordinarily rapid social and technological progress; but the nineteenth century managed, though with difficulty, to accommodate this change without cataclysm. The managers of the twentieth century had less luck – or less wisdom.

In 1814 the statesmen of Europe gathered in Vienna to put together again their world, which had been shaken to pieces by the French Revolution and Napoleon. This world was by modern standards a narrow one. It was confined to Europe. The world outside Europe, apart from the United States, was for them significant mainly because it contained a number of valuable colonies which were stakes on the table (though not the most important stakes) in the negotiations for a settlement. They were not concerned principally with matters of trade or economy, let alone the environment. They would have been amazed at the thought that these were proper items for the agenda at Vienna. With the partial exception of the British they did not have to concern themselves in any precise way with public opinion in their own countries, let alone in the smaller countries whose future they were deciding. They were concerned with the traditional questions of diplomacy – frontiers, alliances, the survival of dynasties, war and peace.

Yet Metternich, Castlereagh, Talleyrand, Alexander I and the kings assembled at Vienna certainly did not regard their task as easy. On the contrary their world had been shaken so rudely that the responsibility of repairing it weighed on them heavily. While they were still at work the earthquake produced an after-shock in the form of Napoleon's escape from Elba and the Hundred Days which ended at Waterloo. They felt consternation during those days, not because they feared that Napoleon could once again become the ruler of Europe, but because the episode threw a dismal light on their own task. They had put King Louis XVIII of France back on his throne, but keeping him there was clearly not going to be easy. And if that was true of the Bourbons, how about the Hapsburgs, the Hohenzollerns and the rest of them?

The eighteenth century had been full of wars and of peace treaties. As a consequence the concept of a balance of power sustained by alliances became familiar. These had been wars between nations – no longer religious wars as in the past, but not yet the revolutionary wars of the future. Armies fought because their rulers had ambitions and because it seemed in the nature of man to go to war. There was a cheerful cynicism about the making of both peace and war. But at the end of that century the rulers of Europe found themselves threatened not by a French king but by a French Revolution.

When King Charles I was beheaded, that could be regarded as an eccentricity of the violent English. When King Louis XVI lost his head in 1793 the lesson was quite explicitly intended for rulers everywhere – *sic semper tyrannis*. True, there had been an American revolution a few years before, but this was a long way away and seemed on the whole to have been a gentlemanly affair. No one could regard George Washington as a revolutionary, and it was pleasant to see the English discomfited. The rulers of Europe eventually rallied their nations, persuading them that the French were invaders, not liberators. But the combination of French revolutionary fervour and Napoleon's military genius had created dangers which were not laid to rest by his defeat. What had happened before could happen again, and it was the central purpose of the Congress of Vienna to prevent this. The driving intellectual force was provided by Prince Metternich, Foreign Minister of the Austrian Empire. Since Austria ruled over a formidable mix of nationalities it was, of all the European regimes, the most vulnerable to revolution and even democracy.

The Vienna settlement rested on two principles and one procedure. The first principle was the familiar balance of power. Luckily among the Allies there was no overwhelming superior. Austria was by now essentially defensive, Prussia not yet essentially aggressive. Russia disposed of huge armies but there were too many gaps and defects in her society for her to qualify as an overlord of Europe. Britain was by now invincible at sea and her army had fought well in Spain and at Waterloo, but she had neither the instinct nor the power to dominate continental Europe. That left France, which had not only aimed at domination but achieved it. The treatment of France, defeated but essentially still the strongest country in Europe, was crucial to the settlement. If France had been treated in 1814 as Germany was treated in 1918 the history of the nineteenth century might well have been disastrous. But the victors acted with restraint. The crimes of France could be heaped on the banished Emperor Napoleon, and generosity shown to the elderly King Louis returned from exile. France was deprived of the territory seized since the Revolution, but not otherwise humiliated. Before long she was back on equal terms with the other European powers – like Germany in the early 1950s rather than Germany in the 1920s.

The second principle was legitimacy. It was felt essential that kings should be kept on their thrones. Kings themselves had always felt that way. Now their natural desire to cling to power was elevated into a doctrine: indeed not just a political doctrine, but an article of faith. The Czar Alexander I, having passed through various intellectual and spiritual excitements in his life, came towards the end to a mystical belief in a revived Christendom under his leadership. Metternich, being more clever and more cynical, was not himself enthralled by the misty concept of a holy alliance, but his political convictions made him a powerful conservative missionary. He distrusted compromise. He carried realism in politics to its logical conclusion. It was not necessary to enquire into the merits of the King of Naples or Spain or Portugal, or to ask how well their people were governed. The essential need for Europe was peace, and the experience of the last twenty-five years had shown that the greatest threat to peace was revolution. In theory, he might acknowledge that you could have reform without revolution, but the example of Louis XVI showed that in practice the one led to the other. You began with a parliament and ended under the guillotine. The English were different, being rich, an island and incapable of logical thought. It was desirable to bring them as far as possible into the balance of power in Europe, but not if that meant listening to lectures from them on the right of peoples to choose their own government. Once that principle was accepted chaos would again be loosed upon the world.

It was not enough, in the belief of the great powers at Vienna, to establish these principles and to redraw the frontiers. Some machinery was needed to prevent the settlement unravelling. The great powers needed to meet from time to time to review the situation and to concert action against any process that threatened their settlement. In particular it might be necessary to agree on help to be given to the weaker or more foolish brethren among the crowned heads of Europe who might come under pressure to make dangerous concessions to their people. Out of this concept was born the various meetings of the great powers in the decade that followed Waterloo. These meetings became known as the Concert of Europe and were in a muddled sort of way the forerunners of the European summits of today – or perhaps more precisely of the smaller more informal meetings of the larger powers such as the Contact Group that eventually brought peace to Bosnia or the Quadrilateral Meetings, ostensibly about Berlin, that enabled the United States, France, Germany and Britain to discuss important issues of the day without enraging too greatly the governments that were excluded.

In 1919, as we shall see, the United States took the crucial lead in making the peace settlement, but then quickly turned its back on the results. After 1814 there was a similar though slower and less complete withdrawal of Britain from the Concert of Europe and the assumptions that underpinned its work. Lord Castlereagh was the architect of British foreign policy until his suicide in 1822. This intelligent but inarticulate aristocrat was deeply unpopular both in England and Ireland. Yet he was an outstanding Foreign Secretary. To radicals he seemed the embodiment of aristocratic resistance to reform. The denunciation by Shelley in 'The Mask of Anarchy' is well known:

> *I met Murder on the way*
> *He had a mask like Castlereagh*
> *Very smooth he looked yet grim;*
> *Seven blood hounds followed him*
> *All were fat; and well they might*
> *Be in admirable plight,*
> *For one by one, and two by two*
> *He tossed them human hearts to chew*
> *Which from his wide cloak he drew.*

Yet something is amiss in Shelley's portrait. If the portrait were accurate then Castlereagh would have been a fully committed lieutenant of Metternich in enforcing the rule of emperors, kings and aristocracies across Europe. He was indeed an expert diplomatist, as skilled in the arts of private persuasion as he was deficient in public oratory. His long experience and a certain intellectual detachment, combined with the wealth and success of his country, gave him an enviable influence in the courts and meeting places of Europe. His personal relationship with Metternich was good, and he sympathised with Metternich's desire to create what Castlereagh once described as 'the great machine of European safety'. Yet he drew back from associating Britain with that machine and thus weakened it almost as decisively as the American repudiation of the League of Nations weakened that effort after 1919.

Castlereagh's reluctance was partly forced on him by his colleagues. They did not share his knowledge of the intricacies of Europe. They were, however, strongly opposed to anything that permanently entangled Britain in European affairs, particularly the internal turmoil of individual continental states. Castlereagh agreed with his Cabinet colleagues that it could not be in British interests to help the lamentable King of Naples to suppress his own subjects. In Castlereagh's words it was not wise for the European powers to act as 'armed guardians of all thrones'.

Castlereagh's doubts were intensified by his successors Canning and then Palmerston. They had more personal sympathy than Castlereagh with radicals and patriots, whether in Latin America or on the continent of Europe. They adopted the jaunty, pragmatic approach to European intricacies which particularly infuriated their continental contemporaries. These found Palmerston particularly maddening because his flippancy masked a capacity for hard work and a detailed knowledge of European affairs in which he was equal to Castlereagh.

The Vienna settlement was based on realism. It regarded political idealism as dangerous and destructive. It sought to establish a framework of security in Europe that would prevent the powers fighting each other as they had during most of the eighteenth century, but would also prevent the peoples rising against the powers. In neither aim would it be entirely successful. Yet the European wars of the nineteenth century were exceptional and limited in time and scope. Regimes changed, sometimes as in Britain by evolution, sometimes by revolution. Germany and Italy were unified. France moved from a conservative to a liberal monarchy, then to a republic, then to an empire, then to the Third Republic; but none of these changes created in Europe the chaos that followed the first French Revolution. The main elements of the Vienna settlement held. Because of that the nations of Europe put down roots into their own soil and created that solidity which, as Scott Fitzgerald pointed out, made possible the patriotic heroism and thus the interminable suffering of the Great War.

The foundations of this European settlement were undermined long before its collapse by the most intelligent and ruthless practitioner of realism whom Europe has seen in these two centuries. To Otto von Bismarck any concept of European order was valueless. Metternich and Castlereagh, and afterwards in their different ways Disraeli and Gladstone, all believed somewhat vaguely in a concert of Europe designed to secure peace. To Bismarck this was humbug. 'Qui parle Europe a tort, notion geographique,' he said, and on another occasion 'the only healthy foundation for a large state . . . is state egoism rather than romanticism, and it is unworthy of a great state to fight for something which does not concern its own interests.' The prime interest of Bismarck was the unification of Germany under Prussian leadership, and then the buttressing of this united German empire against any possible attack. Germany became what, despite two defeats, she has remained, the strongest country in Europe.

For this cause Bismarck manipulated everybody, including his own king and his own emotions. He preferred tension to harmony. One has the impression that he enjoyed his own vulnerability to rage and despair. He could show forbearance when it suited him, for example in the generous terms shown to Austria after her defeat in 1866, paving the way for the solid alliance that he made with her thirteen years later. He failed to show similar generosity to France after her defeat in the Franco-Prussian War. Indeed he made the same mistake towards France as the French made towards Germany after the Great War. By his treatment of France he created for Germany a permanent enemy, bent on revenge and the recapture of Alsace and Lorraine. To frustrate the French Bismarck built an amazing edifice of secret treaties, contradictory but in the short run effective – with Austria, with Austria and Italy, with Austria and Russia, and finally with Russia separately.

The new young German Kaiser Wilhelm II dismissed Bismarck in 1890. It is sometimes supposed that it was the arrogance and stupidity of the Kaiser that brought Bismarck's subtle system crashing to the ground. Certainly the Kaiser, by refusing to renew the arrangement with Russia, and by challenging Britain to a naval arms race, narrowed Germany's options, forced Russia and France together, and turned Britain from a cautious neutral into a likely enemy. But it is hard to see how the system could have continued in the complicated and contradictory way that Bismarck had devised. It is difficult to deceive all the people all the time. Bismarck was so persistent and ruthless a practitioner of *realpolitik* that he carried realism to the verge of absurdity. His cruder successors pushed Germany and Europe into the abyss, but it was he who brought them to the edge.

Alliances need not have this effect. After the Second World War Europe was again divided into two alliances, this time with the United States whole-heartedly engaged. The Atlantic Alliance was based on a complex theory of deterrence which was constantly discussed and refined. The aim was to guarantee peace by ensuring that the consequences of aggression were intolerable for the aggressor. The alliances constructed at the time of Bismarck and the Kaiser rested on no such doctrine of deterrence. If you had asked Gladstone whether there would ever be another major European war he would have replied truthfully but equivocally that he prayed to God that this would not happen. If you had asked Bismarck he would have mocked the stupidity of the question. Wars in his view should be entered into with care and calculation, and should be ended quickly. But to exclude them as a means of national policy would be absurd. When statesmen entered one or other of the European alliances at the end of the nineteenth century they did so not to prevent war but to ensure that their country was not the loser, if eventually war came.

Bismarck knew something of the brutalities of modern warfare. He was at Sadowa when the Prussians beat the Austrians in 1866 and at Sedan soon after they beat the French in 1870. He knew about the mess, blood and enormous casualties of a modern battle. The French Emperor, Napoleon III, had been present at the Battle of Solferino a few years earlier when his army beat the Austrians out of Lombardy and opened the way for the unification of Italy. Out of that slaughter came the foundation of the International Red Cross. Yet, as often happens, it took time for statesmen and diplomats to realise that the change in the nature of warfare had to affect their own profession. There was no sudden single event like the first atom bomb at Hiroshima to concentrate their attention. The diplomats who handled the aftermath of the Archduke Franz Ferdinand's assassination in June 1914 performed much as their predecessors had done a hundred years before – as if neither railways nor the machine gun had meanwhile been invented.

After that murder in Sarajevo the carefully constructed system of alliances moved smoothly into action. Each party carried through those of its commitments that it thought crucial. Austria used the assassination as a pretext to suppress the nationalist aspirations of the Serbs, which it thought threatened the Hapsburg Empire. Russia moved against Austria to protect Serbia. Germany moved against Russia to protect Austria. Germany moved against France to forestall French action in support of her ally Russia. The diplomats worked to avert the crisis as they had averted several similar crises in recent years. They were handicapped by the preoccupation of the generals with the techniques of mass mobilisation. Once a huge army began to mobilise along the carefully prepared railways it was in practice difficult to arrest its movement into war. The emperors of Germany, Austria and Russia were not themselves professional soldiers. But the uniforms that they wore and the traditions that surrounded them showed where their instincts would lie in any clash between their diplomats and their soldiers.

There was one particularly damaging example of this predominance of the military. The Germans had long planned to outflank the French defences with a wide sweep through neutral Belgium. This made inevitable Britain's early entrance into the war. There was much argument afterwards as to whether Britain would in any case have come into the war even though she had no precise commitment to help France. Probably she would. Secret staff talks had been based on that assumption. The outlook for Britain's security would have been desperate if Germany had managed to knock France out of the war in the autumn of 1914 as she had in 1870 and did again in 1940. But the invasion of Belgium ensured that Britain entered the war at once and with a nation virtually united behind the Asquith Government.

It is often assumed that wars are brought about by soldiers and militarist elites, but never by democracies. There is obviously some truth in this. Democratic politicians know that they will be held personally to account by those whose husbands and children are sent to war. Henry Kissinger makes the point that the argument was strongest when applied to industrial democracies, where the citizen had a substantial stake to lose in war. Prosperity is certainly a force for peace. Yet the 1914 war was initially as popular in Britain and France, with their prosperous establishments of classes and their democratic governments, as it was in Germany, Austria and Russia.

Prosperity does not always act against violence – or at least, not quickly. Northern Ireland has a strongly established professional middle class and has for years now seen a gradual growth in prosperity. Yet until 1998 that co-existed with terrorism and communal violence. At last, seventy-six years after partition, it looks as though people feel they have a stake in that province to prevent it being torn apart again by terrorism.

The initial enthusiasm for the war evaporated as the military stalemate set in and the casualty lists grew. But growing pessimism did not have the effect on popular opinion that might have been expected, except in Russia. There was no serious pressure for a compromise peace. Indeed when the distinguished and traditional British Lord Lansdowne, former Foreign Secretary and Viceroy of India, proposed a negotiated peace in 1917 he gained little popular support. It was as if the mounting pile of corpses were extra stakes on the table. Precisely because the sacrifice was proving so much greater than anyone had expected, the need for unmistakable victory became absolute – a victory that would have to be followed by a peace settlement which made sure that this never happened again.

That feeling would have been strong in Europe in any case once the fighting ceased. But it was given enormous power and popularity by the President of the United States, Woodrow Wilson. In clear, eloquent language he expressed what millions felt. Here was a new figure with a new voice and a new message. Woodrow Wilson had brought the United States very reluctantly into the war eighteen months before it ended. By this act he had ensured that in the end the Allies would win. But he also made it clear that he was fighting a different war from that being waged by his allies and would seek a different kind of peace. As Henry Kissinger put it in his masterly analysis, *Diplomacy*, 'Amidst the rubble and the disillusionment of three years of carnage, America stepped into the international arena with a confidence, a power and an idealism that were unimaginable to its more jaded European allies.'

Woodrow Wilson had not waited for the end of the war to proclaim his message. The Fourteen Points he announced in January 1918 had at their heart a simple, strong set of ideas. It is hard to imagine anything more radical. The balance of power was roundly rejected as a basis for international peace. Instead there needed to be 'a community of power, not organised rivalries, but an organised common peace'. This common peace must be based on the principle of self-determination.

Every people should be left free to determine its own policy, its own way of development, unhindered, unthreatened, unafraid, the little along with the great and the powerful.

No peace can last which does not recognise and accept the principles that governments derive all their powers from the consent of the governed and that no rights exist to hand peoples from sovereignty to sovereignty as if they were property.

Because nations would now be planning for peace not for war their plans must include substantial disarmament so that the strong could no longer threaten the weak. The settlement should be based on the principle of collective security. Alliances between particular nations should be replaced by a League of all nations, relying not on armaments but on the force of democratic public opinion to deter and check anyone tempted to aggression.

The bedrock of this approach was that mankind is good. Left to themselves democratic nations would live peacefully together, because that is the nature of humanity. Wars had been caused by the distortion of that underlying goodness. Secrecy, privilege, old-fashioned diplomacy, imperialism – these were the ancient vices and distortions that had led the world into cataclysm and must now be discarded.

There was nothing new about the doctrine of the perfectibility of man. In different forms it came down through Rousseau, Tom Paine and indeed Marx. The thought has continued to be a commonplace in the mouths of statesmen in democratic countries. What was new in 1918 and 1919 was the spectacle of the most powerful man in the world actually insisting that this principle and its consequences should be put into practice. There were no precedents for this spectacle, and it has never been repeated with such power. As H.G. Wells noted:

For a brief interval Wilson stood alone for mankind . . . he was transfigured in the eyes of men. He ceased to be a common statesman. He became a messiah . . . millions believed him as the bringer of untold blessings. Thousands would have died for him.

Much of the strength of Woodrow Wilson's ideas derived from the fact that he was an American. In practice, United States policy through the nineteenth century had been isolationist rather than idealist. It was a historical flaw in Woodrow Wilson's Fourteen Points when he compared them to the Monroe Doctrine. The Monroe Doctrine certainly warned the old European powers against interference on the American continent, but these warnings were not held to apply to the United States itself. The Fourteen Points must have come as a bit of a surprise to those in Mexico and Central America who were familiar with the presence of US marines, but not with the principles of self-determination. Nor indeed had the Southern States been allowed self-determination at the time of the Civil War. Nevertheless such historical quibbles were swept aside by the sheer strength of American idealism. It was as if America had kept herself ready for this moment, when she could intervene decisively on the world stage, not just with troops but with the full force of American principles. This was certainly how her President felt. It was this thought that roused him to his most poetic eloquence.

America has been cried awake by these voices in the disturbed and reddened night, when fire sweeps sullenly from continent to continent.

And it may be that in this red-flavoured night there will rise again that ideal figure of America holding up her hand of hope and guidance to the people of the world.

Never before or since has idealism in the search for peace been so clearly defined or so forcefully put forward.

This irresistible force came up against an immovable object, namely the realities of the world. The outcome was the Versailles Treaty, which embodied neither idealism nor reality. The settlement began to flake away almost as soon as the treaty was signed. Well-meaning diplomats and statesmen were constantly at work through the 1920s, and more desperately through the 1930s, trying to patch it up and hold it together. It finally collapsed a brief twenty years after its creation.

The Versailles Treaty broke down on a paradox. Germany had been comprehensively defeated in the war, but she had nevertheless replaced victorious France as the most powerful country on the continent of Europe. This was far from clear in 1919, particularly to the British, some of whom even thought and wrote of France as a potential enemy all over again. But the facts of population and economic strength were inexorable. The Allied powers could have followed either one of two logical courses. They could have created a generous peace, bringing a democratic Germany as quickly as possible back into the international community and heaping all the blame for the past on the exiled Kaiser. Or they could have maintained a punitive peace, setting themselves decade by decade to offset Germany's strengths with economic and military penalties and controls.

Seasoned politicians like Lloyd George and Balfour ruminated in private about the advantages of a generous peace. But they believed that this was not conceivable in terms of public opinion. In public Lloyd George spoke of hanging the Kaiser and squeezing Germany until the pips squeaked. The democratic politicians had much less scope for generosity towards defeated Germany in 1919 than the aristocratic politicians had had towards defeated France in 1814.

Instead the peace was punitive. Germany had to admit moral guilt for the war. She had to pay reparations on a huge, though ill-defined scale. She had not only to restore Alsace Lorraine to France, which was not really a problem, but to allow millions of Germans in the east to pass under Polish and Czech rule. These provisions were clearly at odds with the Fourteen Points of Woodrow Wilson. They contradicted self-determination. They were repugnant to the German people as well as to the German Government and were increasingly felt in Britain and the United States to be unjust. For that reason they fell away quite rapidly in the 1920s. Reparations were slimmed down. Germany was admitted to the League of Nations. It was made fairly clear at Locarno in 1925 that provided Germany recognised the permanence of her western borders there would be scope for her to regain peacefully some of the territories ceded in the east.

The result of the Versailles settlement was thus to create a Germany full of grievances, but not under the kind of consistent control that would prevent her upsetting when she could the treaty which embodied these grievances.

France, the chief practitioner of realism, suffered most severely when realism was thrown out of the window. She had suffered appallingly in the war. Her industrial areas, unlike those of Germany, had been devastated. Her former ally, Russia, had retreated into eastern darkness. Her leaders saw clearly that her salvation must lie in a clear guarantee from Britain and the United States that if France was attacked by Germany they would come to her defence. But this was to talk the language that Woodrow Wilson had repudiated. Woodrow Wilson himself was repudiated by his own people. The United States Congress was not willing to endorse even the flabby undertakings of collective security that Woodrow Wilson was prepared to contemplate under the aegis of a League of Nations. In these circumstances Britain, too, was unwilling to give that firm, practical guarantee followed by military arrangements that France needed. France put together an alliance of the weak new states in Central Europe – Poland, Czechoslovakia, Rumania – but nobody believed that they could play the part in the balance of power which imperial Russia had played before the Great War.

The French were willing to go along with the idealistic rhetoric of the League provided that collective security under the League could be interpreted as guaranteeing their safety. But collective security meant very little in practice unless it could be followed by a practical alliance with military planning to deter and if necessary reverse an act of aggression. The assumption under the League's version of collective security that everyone would rally against any act of aggression meant in practice that no one would rally. Intense diplomatic activity in the decade after Versailles failed to resolve this problem. The high water mark came with the Treaty of Locarno in 1925.

On paper the network of ingenious agreements made at Locarno answered most of the outstanding questions. In practice they were not credible. By accepting their western frontiers as defined at Versailles but refusing to accept the eastern frontiers, the Germans made it clear that they intended to pick and choose between pieces of the treaty that had been imposed upon them. The British, by then in the full tide of pacifist reaction against war, made no pretence of supposing that their undertakings at Locarno should be followed by staff planning or a halt to the rapid disarmament urged at that point by Winston Churchill as Chancellor of the Exchequer. Before Locarno, the French had practised confrontational policies, typified by their strong stand on reparations and their occupation of the Ruhr in 1923. After Locarno they relapsed into a cynical pessimism, building the Maginot Line, but drained of confidence either in their potential adversaries, in their allies, or in themselves.

The Versailles settlement was fundamentally defective. This was not because it was a compromise between idealism and reality. Every peace settlement contains such a compromise. But the Versailles compromise was particularly perverse. The ingenious diplomatic tinkering in the 1920s did not tackle the real deficiencies. The settlement could have deteriorated into untidy confusion and occasional minor conflict. Thanks to the demonic ruthlessness of Adolf Hitler, it collapsed instead into a new cataclysmic world war.

Hitler did not alter the aims of German foreign policy. He inherited the fundamental objective of Stresemann, who signed the Locarno Treaty. Almost all Germans, democrats as well as Nazis, believed that the Versailles Treaty was unjust and must be changed. They wished to see Germany restored to her natural position among European nations. She must be freed of the war guilt clause, of reparations, of one-sided rules on disarmament, and entitled to the same application of the principle of self-determination to Germans as to anyone else. Hitler's change was one of method and pace. He did not want war, but he was perfectly prepared to threaten it and indeed to launch it if necessary to achieve his aims. He was capable of manoeuvre, as his short-lived agreements with Poland, with Britain on naval strengths, and with the Soviet Union, bore witness. He played with great skill on the feeling, particularly strong in Britain, that Germany had been badly treated at Versailles.

Two of the first blows to the international structure of peace came from outside Europe. The Japanese invasion of Manchuria in 1931 was brushed over by the League of Nations as if it had never been. More subversive was the Italian invasion of Abyssinia in 1935. Britain and France rallied the members of the League of Nations to apply sanctions against the aggressor – and then their two foreign ministers put together a scheme for the partition of Abyssinia which public opinion repudiated once it had been leaked. The Hoare-Laval Pact would have left the Emperor Haile Selassie with about half his kingdom. Once it was repudiated, he lost the whole.

After this display of impotence the League of Nations ceased to exercise even moral authority, even among remaining idealists. The British Labour Party, for example, continued to oppose British rearmament on the grounds that aggression must be whole-heartedly opposed, but that this could only be done through the useless collective security provisions of the League. This approach, which had been very widespread, became incredible after the invasion of Abyssinia. Anthony Eden had already warned against supposing that lofty ideals could keep the peace unless matched by a willingness to take realistic measures. Quite quickly the structure created at Versailles collapsed. Those concerned were reduced to scrabbling about among the ruins for such bits and pieces of assurance as they could cobble together.

The two following episodes on which historians have rightly focused are the Nazi occupation of the Rhineland in 1936 and the Munich crisis two years later. On both occasions the desperate and demoralised French made warlike noises, consulted London, and let it be known that since Britain would not fight, France could not. On both occasions the French were by no means eager for war, but anxious to shift the responsibility to others. The Rhineland had been demilitarised under the Versailles Treaty. To France its occupation by German troops reduced the practical feasibility of their own alliances with Poland and the Czechs. It was also proof to them of the fundamentally aggressive nature of Nazi Germany. To the British, Hitler was abruptly and reprehensibly correcting a defect in the Versailles Treaty by bringing part of Germany back under full German control.

Suppose that Britain and France had gone to war with Germany when Hitler occupied the Rhineland. It is clear now, whatever they may have thought at the time, that the Allies would have won, since German rearmament was in its infancy. What then? Would they then themselves occupy the Rhineland as the French occupied the Ruhr in 1923? How would they then have dealt with the passive resistance, the continued intransigence of the aggrieved German nation, whether under the leadership of Hitler or some successor? In retrospect one can see that the defeat of Hitler in 1936 might have spared the world the Second World War, but that is not how it seemed at the time.

Writing of this period, A. J. P. Taylor judged:

From this moment until the outbreak of war 'realists' and 'idealists' stood on opposing sides. Practical statesmen, particularly those in power, pursued policies of expediency without thought of principle. Disillusioned idealists refused to believe that the men in power could ever be supported or even entrusted with arms. The few who tried to bridge the gap were in the worst case. Eden, for example, remained Foreign Secretary in order to save something from the wreck; in practice he became simply a cover for the cynical 'elder statesmen' Sam Hoare and Neville Chamberlain. Even Winston Churchill, who talked in high terms of collective security and resistance to aggression, estranged the idealists by talking also of the need for greater British armaments and so remained until the outbreak of war a solitary figure distrusted by both sides. Of course there is always some cleavage between principle and expediency; but it was never so wide as in the four years after December 1935.

I would quarrel only with the inclusion of Neville Chamberlain among the cynics. Certainly when it came to the Munich crisis he behaved intolerably to the Czechs. In his anxiety to avoid war he left them entirely out of the discussions that organised the cession of the Sudetenland to Germany and so ensured their immediate enfeeblement and eventual destruction as a country. But at Munich the idealistic and realistic arguments became mixed up. Chamberlain and the millions across the world who supported him could argue that the Germans who were living in Czechoslovakia were morally entitled to the self-determination that Woodrow Wilson had promised to all. It was the realists who argued that to rob Czechoslovakia of her natural mountain frontiers was to alter unacceptably the balance of power in Central Europe. Which side would Woodrow Wilson have taken at Munich? Would he have argued for self-determination or for the balance of power?

But the merits of the Czech and German arguments were not at the forefront of Chamberlain's mind. Nor was he playing for time, recognising that war was inevitable but aiming to postpone it to allow Britain's rearmament to gather strength. It is true and to Chamberlain's credit that the year of peace gained between 1938 and 1939 was well used to build up the Royal Air Force and introduce conscription. But Chamberlain was driven primarily by a determination to avoid war if at all possible, and only secondarily by the need to win it if it came. War, whether it ended in defeat or once again in victory, was the evil. He could not begin to share Churchill's underlying excitement at questions of strategy and military leadership. The shadow of the slaughter of the Great War hung over him as over so many – perhaps all the more because he himself had not fought in it. Anthony Eden, Harold Macmillan, Duff Cooper and a handful of other politicians had actually fought in the trenches and came to realise at different times during the late 1930s that another war was becoming inevitable. Chamberlain, like most of his fellow citizens, was reluctant all the way – which is why each of Britain's decisions came too late. There was blindness and stubbornness here, but not cynicism. The system of Versailles had collapsed, and there was no place of safety among the ruins, only moral and intellectual confusion.

If we use the benefit of hindsight this fearful deterioration could conceivably have been arrested, perhaps about the year 1928. If at that time, before the great slump, before Hitler arrived in power, a fundamental reshaping of the Versailles settlement had taken place, the outcome could have been different. This would have meant extending to Germany a generosity ten years after the Great War such as she received four years after the Second War. This would have involved the cancellation of all reparations, the removal of the war guilt clause, permission to rearm within limits and some revision of her eastern frontiers to include more Germans in Germany. At the same time, and crucially, there would have had to be a firm

Anglo-French alliance, with a published security guarantee and a joint structure for military action. Conceivably a new balance of power might thus have been created in Europe.

Even to sketch this, however, is to show how unrealistic such a proposal would have been. Woodrow Wilson achieved his temporary supremacy because of the huge enthusiasm of people behind him, in Europe as well as America. Public opinion was, he thought, his ally against the old-fashioned principalities and powers. Yet it was public opinion which in the end undermined the Treaty of Versailles and the concept of collective security by paralysing the will of democratic statesmen. No one can say that Baldwin or Chamberlain or the politicians of the Third Republic in France made stalwart efforts to change public opinion, which was a strange mixture of empty illusions and cynical pessimism. The politicians were too much subject to these emotions themselves to be capable of giving a strong lead away from them. The reaction when it came was swift and strong. Baldwin and Chamberlain were execrated later for carrying out the policies which at the time the people required. But an important lesson was also learned. When in the 1940s and again in the 1970s it was necessary to rally public opinion to be ready to withstand aggression and resist the blandishments of unilateral disarmament, Western leaders were hugely helped by over-simplified memories of the 1930s, leading to the conclusion that weak wills were dangerous and appeasement a dirty word.

CHAPTER TWO

1945 – 1956

Whe n the President of the United States, Franklin Delano Roosevelt, left in February 1945 for his last international mission at the Conference in Yalta in the Crimea, there was an uncanny resemblance between the ideas and prejudices in his baggage and those carried to Europe by his predecessor Woodrow Wilson in 1919. FDR was a shrewder and more worldly politician than Woodrow Wilson. He was much more experienced in international affairs. But he retained to the end the same conviction as Woodrow Wilson, that America must use her strength to bring into being a new radical world order based on particularly American virtues of democracy and justice.

The Crimean Conference ought to spell the end of the system of unilateral action, the exclusive alliance, the spheres of influence, the balance of power, and all the other expedients that have been tried for centuries and have always failed. We propose to substitute for all these a universal organisation in which all peace-loving nations will finally have a chance to join.

These are the words of Roosevelt in 1945; they could without any alteration have been used by Woodrow Wilson in 1918.

There had, however, been one important step forward in American thinking. FDR did not believe, like Woodrow Wilson, that the force of democratic public opinion would be enough to sustain the League of Nations and frustrate any future aggressor. He accepted that his new world order would need to be policed. As policemen he saw no alternative to the four main victorious allied powers – the United States, the Soviet Union, Britain and China. In return for accepting the role of policemen the great powers could be reasonably sure that the force of the new United Nations would not be turned against them. So with their special responsibilities went a veto in the new Security Council of the United Nations. By the time the UN was set up at San Francisco in the summer of 1945 the four had become five. Roosevelt's experiences with General de Gaulle in the war left him unenthusiastic about post-war France, but with Churchill's strong support France found her way to the top table when the UN Charter was actually drawn up.

There were two difficulties about this concept of policemen. The first was that two of the four policemen were on sick-leave. China was absorbed in the Civil War between the Nationalist Government of Chiang Kai-shek and the Chinese Communists. Britain, though outwardly triumphant and back in possession of the biggest empire in the world, was in dire financial difficulties and within a few years of losing that empire. The confidence which, for the first two years after the war, the Americans placed in Britain's continued strength was remarkable. They seriously believed that Britain was capable of providing, without American help, for the security of Western Europe from which American troops would be withdrawn. This is the more odd since in another strand of policy the Americans were anxious that the British, French and other colonial empires should be dismantled. They were also suspicious when Britain assumed in Greece at the end of the war precisely the thankless task of a policeman on part of his beat.

But the main defect in Roosevelt's scheme was the total lack of harmony between the two most powerful policemen. Stalin was not, like Hitler, possessed by demons. As a convinced Communist he no doubt believed that the eventual success of Communist revolutions across the world would establish the Soviet Union as the dominant world power. But his main concern lay much closer to home. He was determined to establish a solid sphere of influence around the Soviet Union so that it could never again be attacked. To someone of his ruthless cast of mind a sphere of influence meant countries that, whatever their international status, were in fact entirely under his command. They were to be satellites that revolved around Moscow, obedient to laws of physics decreed by the Kremlin. Even when German troops were at the gates of Moscow in December 1941, Stalin, in discussions with Anthony Eden, began to prepare for the post-war settlement. As the Red Army first withstood the Germans, then turned the tide, then caused their own tide to flow over Central Europe, Stalin's definition of the Soviet sphere of influence became wider and more absolute. To the end of his life, Roosevelt did not take this seriously. He believed that the Soviet determination was less important than the relationship which he believed he had established with Stalin as one good policeman with another.

These mists of illusion were quickly blown away after the death of Roosevelt in the spring of 1945 and the victory in Europe a few weeks later. When the Allies met again at Potsdam in June 1945 their biggest difficulty was not (as in 1919) how to deal with the defeated Germany. Indeed that problem was substantially simpler than it had been. This time the Germans had been thoroughly and undeniably defeated in the field. There could be no revival of the old post-1918 argument (so useful to Hitler) that the German army had not been fairly defeated but undermined by disloyal sabotage at home. Moreover, this time there could be no doubt about German war guilt. Historians continue to argue about the share of war guilt carried by Germany in the events of 1914. No one can seriously doubt that the German Führer was the man responsible for war in 1939. The partition of Germany into occupation zones was inevitable and the Germans had neither the power nor the will to resist it. The good sense of the three Western Allies in administering those zones and after a time permitting the amazing revival of German self-confidence through economic success meant that the German problem, though it still exists, took a much more benign form after 1945 than after 1918. The Soviet Union, by creating a model Communist state out of its own occupation zone, ensured for the East Germans ruthless suppression of rights while Communism survived, and deep-seated disadvantage compared to the rest of Germany long after Communism was swept away.

Churchill was dismissed from office by the British people in the General Election of 1945 before the Potsdam Conference reached its conclusions. He believed later that it would have been possible then to prevent Stalin from establishing his grip across Central and Eastern Europe. Certainly the Potsdam settlement, as many Americans admitted privately, was a repudiation of the ideals with which FDR had launched the discussion of a post-war world. The lines of military demarcation between the victorious allied armies were not yet set fast, and there were still non-Communist politicians in countries that later became totally subservient to Moscow. Maybe an Anglo-American ultimatum to Stalin in the summer of 1945 would have caused him to draw back from imposing his will totally on Poland, Hungary and Czechoslovakia. Stalin was calculating, but not mad. If he had encountered stiff resistance at Yalta or at Potsdam he would have paused to calculate. But it is hard to see how calculation would have led him to draw back. His armies had swept into the areas which he believed the Soviet Union must control, whereas the Allied armies at American insistence had not played politics with territory in the final months of the war. Stalin was not interested in economic help to reconstruct his country, as he showed later when rejecting the Marshall Plan. To him Western help meant Western infiltration. Even as the war ended the Communist Party of the Soviet Union was explaining in the factories and the schools that their country's alliance with the West had been fortuitous and that the Western powers were as fundamentally opposed to Communism as the Nazis and Fascists had been.

Nor would the democracies have found it at all easy to persuade their peoples, with Hitler and Mussolini dead, that they now had to face fresh anxieties and risks in order to frustrate the Soviet ally who had fought with such bravery and sacrifice alongside them to win the war. Wartime memories were recent and hugely powerful. For Britain, for example, it would hardly have been possible to act as if the Arctic convoys and the Sword of Stalingrad were a lie.

The democracies were reluctant to describe accurately the unpalatable facts that had thus been created on the ground. A hush of disapproval greeted the declaration by Churchill at Fulton in 1946 that an iron curtain had fallen across Europe. Meanwhile the Soviet Union completed its absorption of its satellites. The ideals proclaimed in the United Nations Charter were virtually extinct in a substantial number of its member states. The United Nations Security Council was paralysed by the veto that the Charter had given to those who were supposed to be the policemen. In these circumstances many people in the West preferred to delude themselves about the nature of Communism and the ruthlessness of Stalin. To those who did not delude themselves, the post-war settlement contained a deep moral flaw, which most accepted as inevitable.

There followed an astonishing paradox. Despite this flaw, or partly because of it, the years between 1947 and 1956 showed a remarkable flowering of constructive statesmanship. Indeed, no decade between 1814 and the present time has proved so productive. Realism and idealism reached the right balance and combined to produce a rich harvest. The Marshall Plan made possible the economic reconstruction of Europe, contrasting vividly with the bickerings about reparations in the 1920s which led to the great slump. The Truman Doctrine reversed the political disengagement of the United States of America from Europe. The United States came to accept the doctrine of containment famously expounded in 1947 by their Ambassador in Moscow George Kennan. This did not imply approval of the

Soviet Union; indeed, it foresaw that over time Communism would fail. But it placed the emphasis on preventing its spread by ensuring the success of the democratic alternative.

NATO was formed to guarantee the security of Western Europe by enlisting permanently on its side the strength of the United States and Canada. Undertakings were given that amounted to a formidable pooling of sovereignty on a scale that could not have been contemplated before, or indeed perhaps since. Britain, for example, which in recent years has been remarkably prickly on matters of sovereignty, committed itself to station British troops in Germany, to join an integrated military system under foreign command, and to go to war instantly if its allies were attacked. Britain accepted these limitations on her freedom without any of the complex reservations and procedures that were later attached to less significant pooling of sovereignty in economic matters.

British statesmanship was well to the fore in this almost miraculous decade. Ernest Bevin as Foreign Secretary took the lead in working out the European response to Marshall, and was one of the main architects of NATO. Anthony Eden put together the Western European Union as a European defence entity. But British wisdom failed when confronted with the final contribution to the harvest. Although Winston Churchill had taken the lead in 1946 in urging France and Germany to come together and in speaking of a United States of Europe, the British Government nine years later did not welcome the outcome of this line of thinking. Confronted with the plan of the six founding fathers of the European Community, the British took a patronising and foolish line, believing that the project was unlikely to succeed and that in any case it was not something in which Britain could or need join.

The foundation of the European Community certainly stands in line as the last of the great initiatives which ensured that, despite the Soviet Union and the threat of Communism, the peace settlement after 1945 lasted longer and produced better benefits for the peoples of Europe than its predecessor after 1918. Much is due to the individual statesmen who, despite the harsh pressures of the moment, looked to the longer term. Much also is due to the increased maturity of public opinion in the democracies which they led, particularly the United States. There was no retreat to isolationism or xenophobia. There was no reaction against the sufferings of the Second World War to match the eloquent but in the end destructive denunciations of war and traditional diplomacy that followed the First World War and helped to ensure that there was a second.

It was I suppose in 1942 that I began as a schoolboy to move flags on the war map on the wall of my room at Eton and to take a daily interest in what was happening in the world. This is not a book about British foreign policy, let alone an auto-biography. Up to now I have treated Britain as just one of many countries involved in the search for peace. If from now on a more personal tone creeps into the narrative from time to time I hope that this may be forgiven. I am still a little way from writing any memoirs and will try to confine myself here to episodes and emotions that can throw some light on Britain's part in the search for peace.

Of those war maps on the wall of my bedroom the most interesting and dramatic was certainly the map of the Western Desert. The campaigns there between 1940 and 1943 were easy to understand and, equally important for a schoolboy, they offered the first good news that we had from any war front. I can remember the names of tiny villages, Sollum, Fort Cappuzzo, as well as of Tobruk, Benghazi and of course El Alamein much more vividly than I can the huge battlefields on the eastern front or indeed later in France and the Low Countries. The British part in the victory parade at Tunis after the Germans and Italians had been driven from Africa in 1943 has been memorably described by Harold Macmillan in a passage worth quoting in full.

The Americans marched well and got great applause, and everyone seemed happy and pleased.

By that time an hour or more had passed and I thought that we would have a small British detachment and then all would be over. But for once the British had decided to put on a really dramatic display which would take everyone by surprise. After the Americans had passed there was a slight pause. Then, coming from far off, a faint sound of pipes. Somebody had collected together all the available pipers from the First and Eighth Armies. Scots Guards, Irish Guards and all the Highland Regiments were represented. When they approached the saluting base they broke into slow time. Then they countermarched – each line wheeling and passing through – one of the most effective of all drills, and then in due course broke into quick time and marched away into the distance with the sound of pipes gradually dying away. Another pause, just long enough for us to wonder whether there had been some hitch; and then the British Army marched past, 14,000 men in all, each division and brigade led by its general and his staff, each battalion by its colonel.

In a long file they came, formation after formation, regiment after regiment, unit after unit.

Unlike the French and Americans the British were in drill, not battle, order – shorts, stockings and boots, battle blouses or shirts with short sleeves – no helmets (forage caps and berets). The helmet gives a soldier the look of a robot . . . With the forage cap or beret you can see his face – his jolly honest, sunburnt, smiling English, Scottish or Irish face – relaxed now, not worn or harassed as men look in battle – and confident and proud. All these brown faces, these brown bare arms and knees, these swinging striding outstepping men – all marched magnificently.

Just before the saluting base (a very old parade trick) there was stationed a band. This of course got all the men marching at their best before they reached the saluting point. My mind went back to Kitchener's Army and the Battle of the Somme. I had always thought that these were the finest British formations that had ever taken the field. But now I had to admit that the First and Eighth Armies were just as good. These men seemed on that day masters of the world and heirs of the future.

That was, I think, the spirit in which many, perhaps most of us celebrated the end of the war in Europe in May 1945. Although we were schoolboys we did not need telling about the cost of war. As we gathered in School Yard for a half-riotous celebration we could see the crater surrounded by willow herb that had once been half of School Hall before the bomb fell in December 1940. The names of recent casualties were read out in chapel at Evensong every Sunday. Earlier names surrounded us in the memorials on the cloister walls – memorials the more touching because they were not some huge assembled total, but different tablets with different designs and different wording to commemorate the fallen of particular families. There was absolutely no glorification of war. On the other hand, this had been an honourable war and Britain, perhaps more than any other country, had taken an honourable part. The deceits and uncertainties of pre-war diplomacy were forgotten. Some of our allies had been defeated or surrendered. The two most powerful, the Americans and the Soviet Union, had arrived on the scene late and only when they had been themselves attacked. They were to be praised and congratulated, not criticised, but we were in a slightly different and higher category. We had stood alone. 1940 was a year we would never forget.

Cheering schoolboys do not worry much about the balance between realism and idealism. There were many things we did not know that day. We did not understand the full horror that the Nazis had inflicted on Europe. The pictures of Buchenwald and Auschwitz were still to come. We did not understand the nature of Communism or the character of Stalin. We did not understand the extent of our own country's impoverishment and the austerity still to come. Bread was rationed in Britain for the first time after the war as a response not to German U-boats, but to the balance of payments. But though we were ignorant of important things I do not believe that we were naive or supposed that victory was a prelude to an inevitable era of settled peace with justice. There was no Woodrow Wilson in 1945 to fire us with a vision of a new heaven and a new earth. We knew enough, I think, to know that nothing was going to be easy. But certainly Britain would play a high and honourable part in peace as in war.

When I joined the Foreign Office in 1952 the mood had changed. This was not just the change from a giddy fifteen to the ripe old age of twenty-two.

By the early 1950s the institutions that were to provide a sound foundation for Britain's future were already taking shape. Not many in Britain understood how fundamental they were to prove for us. Certainly it was already clear that the decline from empire had begun. There would never again be a parade of fighting soldiers such as Macmillan had witnessed in Tunis in 1943. By the time I joined the Foreign Office India had already gone, though (because of oil) the territories in the Middle East which had formerly been important only as staging posts to India were now thought to be crucial in their own right – Egypt, Iran, the Gulf. The change in India was hugely dramatic for the peoples of the sub-continent and of course also for those in Britain whose lives had been shaped by the Raj. But there was less surprise and shock in Britain itself than might have been expected from so tremendous an event. The real change of perception in the first decade after the end of the war was economic. Despite the austerity imposed by the Attlee Government Britain was assailed at irregular intervals by financial crises. The exhaustion that had been concealed during the war became evident to all. Britain took the wrong path after 1945, believing that the mobilisation of state power which had been effective in winning the war would be equally effective in mastering the problems of peace. Too much effort was spent in regulating existing resources fairly and too little in encouraging the private sector to create fresh resources. Consequently British recovery was hampered by inflation and the increase of a backward-looking trade union power. She thus increasingly fell behind those on the continent and in particular the Germans who started from scratch but chose a wiser path based on a modern trade union system (partly designed in Britain) and the encouragement of the private sector. It was evident that whatever the party label of the British Government, the job of its diplomatic service was to manage as skilfully as possible a process of steady decline.

This did not mean that our influence was at an end. On the contrary. There were occasions when diplomatic skill seemed to compensate for increasing poverty.

Two shining examples of this aptitude came close on each other's heels in 1954. In the spring of that year I was posted to Peking and allowed to travel slowly on a French liner from Marseilles to Hong Kong, pausing at Saigon, the capital of French Indo-China. The SS *Cambodge* was full of French troops going to fight in Indo-China against the Communist rebels led by Ho Chi Minh. As we sailed through the Mediterranean, then the Suez Canal, then the Red Sea, the ship's notice-board carried each day bulletins reporting the siege of Dien Bien Phu, the fortress which the French had deliberately created in order to draw the Vietnamese rebels to battle. The news was of passionate interest to almost everyone on board. Eventually we sailed up the Mekong River to Saigon. The troops marched ashore as the band on the quayside played the 'Marseillaise', and ladies on the upper deck dabbed their eyes with lace handkerchiefs. The French as well as the British found many moving moments in the decline of the empire. We stayed three days in Saigon. I slept under a mosquito net, and listened to the crump of mortars as the Vietnamese rebels harassed the suburbs of the capital through the night. It seems a long time ago.

Then we sailed eastwards again, and again gathered round the ship's notice-board. What the notice-board did not carry was any report of the secret diplomacy being conducted at the same time. The American Secretary of State, John Foster Dulles, was preparing to intervene militarily on the side of the French in order, as he saw it, to prevent the on-rush of Communism into South-East Asia. The domino theory, that if one Asian country fell the others would quickly and disastrously follow suit, was already alive and flourishing in the 1950s. But in order to gain the necessary support in Congress Dulles had to persuade his allies, and in particular the British, to join in. The Foreign Secretary, Anthony Eden, quietly but firmly resisted this pressure. He had been desperately ill the year before, but appeared to have fully recovered. He was a figure whom we young diplomats admired immensely, even though in those days young men at the Foreign Office saw little or nothing of their chief. His reputation for charm and courtesy was formidable. His courage had been proved by his resignation from the Chamberlain Government in 1938. He was the heir to the ageing Prime Minister Winston Churchill. We now know that at this time his dealings with Churchill were far from easy. As a professional he disliked the Prime Minister's enthusiasm for ill-defined summit meetings with the Russians, and he was not unreasonably impatient at the repeated delays in Churchill's resignation. But to us he seemed admirable – enormously experienced, articulate in a silvery way, well dressed and almost always right.

Eden was not content with turning down the American proposal for military intervention, which might have included nuclear weapons. He chaired with the Russians the conference at Geneva that brought the Chinese Communists under Chou en Lai for the first time on to the international scene and resulted in the agreement which, for the time being, ended the Vietnam War. By that time I was in our embassy in Peking, sweatily deciphering night by night the immense telegrams repeated to us from Geneva recording the different formulae of the diplomatic exchanges that were preserving the world from war. Although we wished his telegrams could be briefer we felt that our Secretary of State was doing a good job.

Two months after the Geneva Agreement on Indo-China

Anthony Eden faced a new crisis, this time in Europe. Like most people in Britain he had failed to grasp the importance of the movement towards European unity, even though this had been to a large extent signposted by Winston Churchill in his post-war speeches. Eden had angered the more pro-European members of the Cabinet when he made it clear that Britain would not be part of the European Defence Community which appeared to be taking shape. But when the French Parliament put an abrupt end to that project Eden took the lead in the ensuing crisis. Once again his persistence and charm in private dealings brought Americans and Europeans together. Germany was admitted to NATO, the Western European Union was founded, and as a crucial component of the diplomatic success Britain promised to keep the British Army of the Rhine permanently in Germany at a strength of 55,000 men.

These diplomatic triumphs made surprising, even incomprehensible, to many of us the disaster that followed two years later. Eden was by now Prime Minister and running into heavy weather. The nationalisation of the Suez Canal Company by President Nasser of Egypt in July 1956 was certainly a heavy blow. Even though we no longer ruled India it was generally agreed that neither Britain nor France could accept that the power to block our trade routes through the Canal should rest in the hands of a hostile dictator. Once again I was, in the smallest possible way, a witness of what followed, this time as a junior diplomat in the British mission to the United Nations in New York. This is not the place to describe the details of those dismal days and nights, when we saw the position that Britain had patiently built up over the years at the United Nations destroyed. More important, the close and almost automatic co-operation between the British and American Governments on all international matters began to disintegrate in distrust.

The Soviet Union was able to destroy the Hungarian Rising with tanks while the world focused on Suez. It was clear that we were paying, hour by hour, a mounting price for the Anglo-French expedition against Egypt, and even more for the collusion with the Israelis. On instructions we denied this collusion. For a time we believed the denials, but no one even then believed us. Naively I assumed, like many others, that our disgrace was regarded in London as an acceptable penalty to win a great prize. But what was the prize? What was the plan? What was the ending at which we aimed? The immediate effect of our action was to close the Suez Canal, although our main purpose had been to ensure that it stayed open. We had no plan to take over again the government of Egypt; but unless we were prepared to do this any gains made by our armed forces were bound to be transitory. Anthony Eden had begun by portraying Nasser accurately as a demagogic nationalist, who had to be carefully watched, but with whom one could, if necessary, do business. After the nationalisation of the Canal he drew a parallel between Nasser and Hitler which clearly made no sense. But it illuminated why Anthony Eden, the master of diplomacy, persuaded himself to abandon diplomacy in favour of an ill-planned and irrational use of force.

The repair work took a long time. The Suez Crisis tore the veil away from certain pretences. It showed that Britain and France were not great powers in the same league as the United States and the Soviet Union. It showed the limits of the Anglo-American relationship. It showed the relationship between money and power. It also showed the usefulness of the United Nations as an organisation that, under skilled leadership, could rescue the world from a serious predicament.

Dag Hammarskjöld, then Secretary-General of the United Nations, was, I thought and think, a great man. By this I mean that he combined integrity with ability and made the mixture effective. He was emphatically European in his diplomatic instincts, and owed his position quite largely to the efforts of Britain and France. This gave an edge of personal embarrassment to the Suez Crisis, as if he had found the two prefects of the school whom he particularly admired with their fingers in the till. At least until the close of his career he was cautious in action, and sometimes disguised his intentions in a cloud of philosophical language pronounced with a heavy Swedish accent. But he genuinely believed that there was a moral element in international affairs, that the rule of law was imperative, and that these two principles ought to find effective expression in the UN.

He created an idea of the United Nations as something finer and potentially more effective than the interests of its individual members. The whole could be greater than the sum of the parts. Hammarskjöld made mistakes. We found him exasperating at the time of Suez, even though as we grumbled we were seizing the spar that he was holding out in an effort to rescue us from our mistakes. Later he became somewhat too grand, never in his personal dealings for he was without pomp or exaggerated sense of protocol, but in his philosophical claims for the organisation that he led. But those who believe that there is no scope for idealistic leadership in a realistic analysis of missions of peace and war would do well to study the career of Dag Hammarskjöld. The United Nations has survived many disappointments because of the stamp that he left on it.

CHAPTER THREE

1956 – 1997

Previous page *American troops move cautiously through the Vietnam jungle, fearful of Viet Cong ambushes. The Communist enemy proved to be tenacious and skilled in jungle guerrilla warfare, entangling American forces for nearly a decade.*
Camera Press Ltd

By this time the world as a whole was locked into the pattern of the Cold War, which did not change in its essentials for forty years. Neither of the two armed camps seriously wanted to wage war on the other. Each worked hard to undermine the other at home and to strengthen its own position in the uncommitted Third World. Paradoxically the weaker system was the more aggressive. It is impossible to believe that either Stalin or his successors were Marxist idealists like, say, the young men who went to fight from Britain and other countries for the Republican side in Spain during the civil war of the 1930s. But the Soviet leaders were highly skilled in using Marxism as a dynamic missionary force. They convinced many in the West and in the uncommitted world that their philosophy was morally superior, and that they were eventually sure to succeed.

The European colonial powers dismantled their empires with remarkable speed, but not of course fast enough for the nationalist leaders in the countries concerned. The Soviet leaders managed to appear anti-colonialist while doing nothing to dismantle their own rule over non-Russian peoples. In the West the contrast was stark between the democratic rights enjoyed by, say, the electorates of Britain and France, and the colonial regimes of their overseas subjects. In the Soviet Union, no oceans separated ruler and ruled on the map. Since everyone was exploited the exploitation of the non-Russians was hardly remarked, except by themselves. The apartheid regime of South Africa was fastened on as uniquely evil in the world. The anti-apartheid cause united the Communists with the Third World while it embarrassed and divided the West. The warts and disfigurements of American society were displayed for all to see. By contrast, the cosmetic arts have never been so well displayed as in concealing the political and economic diseases that were eating away at the substance of the Communist societies. This combination of factors enabled the weaker and nastier of the adversaries more or less to hold its own for forty years.

These were not easy years for idealists in the West. Woodrow Wilson had launched a peace settlement based on the League of Nations which quickly clashed with reality and failed to work. By contrast at Yalta and Potsdam the victorious Allies had put together a settlement based on reality that *did* work – but at a price. The idealistic wording of the United Nations Charter was put into cold storage. Not even Dag Hammarskjöld was able to prevent the attitudes of the Cold War from dominating the life of the international community. Yet the years of the Cold War were not for most citizens of the West unhappy years.

On the contrary, they were highly successful. The Western economies revived after the war with surprising speed. Even Britain, which was led by the Attlee Government down the wrong path, managed eventually to retrace its steps and rid itself of double digit inflation and trade union power before these became immovable parts of the British scene. NATO and the European Community flourished, though the attempt to breed similar military alliances out of NATO in the Middle East and South East Asia were failures. With some mistakes and setbacks, the process of decolonisation went surprisingly well. The United States continued to flourish and abound.

Against this background the idealists had two main worries, both of them genuine. They worried first and foremost about danger. Western security rested on the theory of deterrence. The Soviet Union could not be trusted to refrain from attacking the West unless the cost to itself of doing so was obvious and overwhelming. Provided NATO remained strong, self-interest would prevent the Soviet Union pushing beyond a certain point. This assumption proved correct. Yet it was only an assumption, not a certainty. If it broke down, the horrors of nuclear war would be upon us. It was inevitable that this policy should be challenged in open debate in the West. The doctrine of deterrence rested on the assumption that the Soviet Union was rational and not demonic like Hitler. It ruled out as negligible the risk of West and East blundering into war through accident. During the forty years of the Cold War there were several moments of acute crisis. I asked some of those responsible for decision-taking during those crises whether they ever felt that the doctrine of deterrence was going to break down and the world hustled into nuclear war. None of them denied that there had been such a moment in their experience.

They gave different examples of when the danger had seemed to them greatest – Berlin 1961, the Middle East 1967, or again 1973 and above all Cuba 1962.

A modern international crisis is fast moving and confused. The speed of modern communications, far from simplifying the issues, tends to complicate them. It increases the number of reports and the number of people who wish to get a word in edgeways. It virtually removes the safety gap between the issuing of an order and its implementation. Anyone who has lived through the centre of a crisis and then later read accounts of it in the newspapers, or from historians, knows how impossible it is to recapture with any fullness the motives and calculations of those involved. Gone are the days of elaborate written documents and carefully recorded conversations. Each crisis generates its own fog of incomplete information, mixed motives and exhaustion. Yet in all the crises of the Cold War sense somehow prevailed through this fog. On the Western side one reason must be the dominance of civilian authority over the military in a Western democracy. Truman was able to sack General MacArthur because he judged that left to himself MacArthur would drive the Korean War out of control. By contrast during the fatal preliminaries to the Great War, the generals of Austria, Germany and Russia had been virtually unsackable. On the Communist side in the Cold War there must have been a still small voice, amid all the noise of their propaganda, reminding those in supreme power that when the chips are down they were vulnerable and likely to lose.

On the Western side the chosen policy of strength and deterrence required resolute leadership and a continuous effort at public education. This had not been required by nineteenth-century leaders after the Treaty of Vienna. It was required, but not attempted by democratic leaders during the 1920s and 1930s until it was too late. It was required and successfully carried through by their successors during the Cold War. Against them were arrayed powerful forces of academic, political and public opinion, exemplified in Britain by the Campaign for Nuclear Disarmament. This was not an argument of Left against Right; indeed some of the most robust proponents of the NATO policy were British Labour and German Social Democrat ministers. The horrors of nuclear war were vivid enough. The risks of a nuclear war could not entirely be denied. As always happens in such arguments, some of those on the better side of the fence used arguments that were callous or foolish. Yet in the end, despite all the marches and demonstrations, the fear of nuclear war did not dominate and then dissolve policy in the same way as fear of a return to the Somme and to Flanders dominated and dissolved policy in the 1920s and 1930s.

There was, however, a shift in Western policy. This would probably have come about anyway, even if there had been no Campaign for Nuclear Disarmament. The concept of massive retaliation put forward by Dulles in the early 1950s implied that any significant Soviet attack upon NATO, even by modest conventional weapons, would be met at once by nuclear retaliation. It was a seductive doctrine to those in possession of nuclear weapons and anxious about the cost of conventional forces. It enabled them to argue that only the deterrents remained of prime importance. But it clearly lacked credibility. It postulated an irrational response out of proportion to the initial offensive action. The successor doctrine of flexible response did not rule out nuclear action, but left it at the end of the range of responses, and it distinguished between tactical and strategic nuclear weapons. It was something of a paradox that this shift to a more sensible doctrine required the biggest battle of all for public opinion over the deployment of Cruise and Pershing missiles in Europe.

The other concern of idealists during the Cold War united traditional liberals with part of the Right in democratic countries. The bargain struck at Yalta and Potsdam was bound to sit uneasily with the idealistic cohort of American opinion. The bargain was not contained in the texts, which were replete with irreproachable statements of principle, but in Western acceptance of facts on the ground. The West did not propose to challenge the realities created by the conquests of the Red Army in 1944 and 1945. They did not effectively oppose the conversion of these military facts into subservient political regimes, creating for Stalin outside the Soviet Union's borders the spheres of brutal influence that he judged essential for its security. It was not open to American Presidents to give in public the practical justification that diplomats could give in private: 'Tough luck. Life is like that. In 1945 we had no alternative.'

To many Americans the only valid questions were whether Communism was good or bad in itself and whether it was good or bad for America. If Communism was bad in both respects then America must fight against it with all means in its power. To shilly-shally on the moral issue was to be un-American. The Yalta-Potsdam Settlement was a revival of the old principle *cuius regio eius religio* which in 1555 helped to settle a ferocious batch of religious wars in Europe. 'The religion of a country is the religion of its ruler.' The popes in Rome were indignant against the settlement of Augsburg on the same grounds as right-wing idealists in America (and at first in Britain) were indignant against the settlement of Yalta–Potsdam. Each implied moral equivalence. Europe was divided in the sixteenth century between Protestants and Catholics, and in the twentieth century between Communists and democrats, as if there was no moral difference between them.

Successive American Presidents of both parties after Truman could not allow this interpretation to stand. Truman, and more particularly his wise Secretary of State, Dean Acheson, despite their achievements were cruelly pilloried by Dulles in the election of 1952 for being content with the doctrine of containment. The critics argued that it was immoral to accept that in certain parts of the world Communist rule had to be tolerated. The Americans should give hope to the captive peoples of Europe, Dulles argued, and work to roll back the frontiers of Communism. It cannot be proved that this kind of rhetoric actually encouraged the people of Hungary to rebel in 1956 in the belief that the US would help them. Some serious observers say it did, though it never occurred to us at the UN during those weeks that the US would intervene militarily to help the Hungarians. Sir William Hayter, our Ambassador in Moscow at the time, believed that had it not been for the coincidence of the Suez Crisis the West might have been able to deter the Russians from sending the tanks to crush Budapest. I doubt it myself. The importance to the Soviet Union of absolute control of their new empire was at that time fundamental.

American Presidents, regardless of party, were not deterred from repeating their rhetoric by this tragedy, or by the similar suppression of the Czechs after the Prague Spring of 1968. President Kennedy's inaugural was in part a hymn to liberty.

*Let every nation know, whether it wishes us well or ill, that we shall
pay any price, bear any burden, meet any hardship, support any friend,
oppose any foe to assure the survival and the success of liberty.*

Ronald Reagan was equally forthright.

*We cannot buy our security, our freedom from the threat of the bomb by
committing an immorality so great as saying to a billion human beings
now in slavery behind the Iron Curtain, 'Give up your dreams of
freedom because to save our own skin, we are willing to make a deal
with your slave-masters.'*

But that deal had been made at Potsdam. When this was denied
or forgotten the gap between rhetoric and reality reopened.

When asked to justify this kind of rhetoric Reagan used to
refer back to his personal experience in Hollywood of Communist agitators in the unions of the American film industry.
One of these whom I interviewed cited this as evidence of
Reagan's superficiality; another as proof of his directness and
honesty. Reagan's personal charm enabled him to combine
such harsh words with courteous personal dealings with Soviet
leaders – even if, as Margaret Thatcher used to complain
affectionately, this courtesy sometimes carried him dangerously
beyond his brief. John Kennedy too, after his eloquence on
liberty, told Americans that they must not fear to negotiate.

As we have seen the military stance of the West was modified
in response to the fear that in its original form it was too
rugged, even dangerous. The same thing happened to its
political stance. The two effective actors in achieving this shift
were Henry Kissinger in the US and Willy Brandt in Germany.
They revived diplomacy, not as a substitute for containment,

but as an aid to it. A slow pattern of arms control agreements began to emerge. The Helsinki Final Act in 1975 gave the Russians in theory what they already had in practice, namely acceptance of the Yalta boundaries. In return they and their allies recognised in treaty form an obligation to respect human rights and thus gave the West a legal right to make representations when this obligation was neglected.

At the time we in the Conservative Opposition in Britain were inclined to dismiss as empty phrases these human rights provisions of the Helsinki Final Act. We were wrong. They gave the West a lever to prise open, slowly and with setbacks, some of the dark shutters of the Soviet system and let in light. During the first part of my time as Foreign Secretary I used to give breakfast to Russian Jewish leaders at the British Embassy when I visited Moscow. They gave me up to the minute briefing that I could use when speaking to the Foreign Minister. Under the Treaty I had the right to name names and leave lists. Gradually the trickle of Jews permitted to leave the Soviet Union became a flow. Later I did not need to continue the breakfasts. I am not suggesting that Western, let alone British, pressures were alone decisive in opening that door or relieving the plight of those who were persecuted. But they certainly helped. Constant drops of water began to wear away the stone.

But before Nixon and Kissinger could make a success of relationships with the Soviet Union they had to extricate the United States from the Vietnam War. Occasionally flawed thinking or a doctrine carried to extreme can pitchfork normally sensible and well-meaning men into a nightmare. In 1914 the damage was done by a blind adherence to the commitments of military alliance without a matching attention to preventive diplomacy; at Suez by a false comparison between President

Nasser of Egypt and the Nazi–Fascist dictators; in Vietnam by exaggerated deference to the theory that any concession to a Communist movement would lead inexorably to the triumph of Communism.

When in interviews for the television series I asked whether the Vietnam policy was the result of realism or idealism, the answer was always blurred. Indeed that is an accurate answer, for the motive was blurred. The South Vietnamese Government was obviously not ideal as a bastion of democracy. Efforts to change it and improve its performance if anything made things worse. But there was no doubt that the Viet Cong were Communists, and once that was established it followed in American eyes that they should be prevented from winning. There was nothing foolish and certainly nothing wicked in that argument. What was amazing was the huge disproportion of the American effort. In all seven and a half million service personnel were involved; more than 57,000 died. The argument destroyed an American President and humiliated America. In the end the Communists won.

To the brief casual visitor Hanoi surprises precisely because there is so little mark of the war. Poverty has so far prevented the Vietnamese from replacing the graceful boulevards and yellow public buildings of the French era with the brash skyscrapers of Bangkok or Hong Kong. Considering the huge casualties and destruction that the Vietnamese on both sides of the war endured, the lack of talk or evidence of war is amazing.

The impact on the US was formidable, yet in the history of America twenty years is a long time. We are not now, thank Heaven, faced with a traumatised nation or a people that has shut itself away from the world to nurse its grief. What remains is caution, a reluctance of President, Congress and people to venture too far. If it had not been for Vietnam, the United States might have continued its intervention in Somalia, despite setbacks. It might have begun an intervention in Bosnia earlier than it did. The allies of America can read this either way. We can welcome the brake that the memory of Vietnam imposes on rash adventures into which the world's remaining superpower might be tempted. Or we can regret that it is now more difficult (though as the Gulf War showed not impossible) for the Americans to accept with energy the risks that go with a world leadership when a crisis occurs. Personally I am sure that it is in our interest to encourage and sustain that American energy.

Much has been written about the circumstances and causes of the collapse of the Soviet Union and its entourage of Communist states. In an analysis Richard Layard and John Parker list three main causes: first the crippling requirements of the defence budget on which the Soviet leaders insisted; second the growing knowledge among the citizens of the Soviet Union that the West, far from collapsing, was steadily growing stronger and more prosperous; third the personality and beliefs of Mr Gorbachev.

It is tempting to go down this last particular byway and speculate how much effect on the course of events is created by individual personalities and their relationships with one another. In normal and diplomatic political life in the West I would guess that personality weighs about one point in the scale against nine points for other relevant factors of strength and weakness. This is a rather lower proportion than the media would give us to suppose because of their preoccupation with matters of personality – but there certainly are occasions when that 10 per cent is enough to tip the scale.

In undemocratic societies, particularly at moments of crisis, the proportion of influence exerted by personality can go much higher. It was certainly so in the Soviet Union after 1985. It is a fascinating testing ground for the relative strengths of idealism and realism in shaping today's world. My own dealings with Gorbachev in 1990 and 1991 did not lead me to suppose that he was an idealist. He seemed a skilful and articulate manager of a decline thrust on him by outside factors, comparable say to Anthony Eden in the 1950s before Suez.

During this time I had four talks with Gorbachev in the Kremlin, three of them alone and the last with the Prime Minister John Major. These talks tended to go on well beyond the allotted time. This was not because we had particularly important matters to negotiate. Gorbachev liked to talk freely to Western ministers, displaying his self-confidence and his mastery of events. He teased his own subordinates, as Stalin had done, though without the sinister undertones. I have a vivid recollection of these discussions. Gorbachev's eyes danced with the sheer enjoyment of his position and the way in which he was mastering the problems that beset him. Even towards the end, when his power was clearly failing, the self-confidence remained. Gorbachev worked by reason and delighted in explaining the line of argument that was guiding his policy. My opinion of him has changed. Two of his closest associates, Shevardnadze and Gerasimov, firmly insisted to me that he was not a realist driven by events, but rather an idealist determined to extricate the Soviet Union from a set of beliefs and policies which he regarded as not only untenable but wrong. These two men worked with Gorbachev day by day and have no particular incentive now for exaggerated praise. Their verdict was supported by George Bush.

Yet the train of reason, even if propelled by idealism, only carried Gorbachev so far. He opened up the Soviet Union. He launched economic reform, he transformed foreign policy and allowed the Soviet satellites their freedom. Yet he never abandoned the belief that the Soviet Union could survive or that the Communist Party could, under his leadership, function as the engine driving reform. It was left to Yeltsin to make these two essential transformations. During this same period I had a number of conversations also with Yeltsin. I noted two opinions in my diary at the time. I thought that Yeltsin would prevail over Gorbachev and that Yeltsin was a dictator in waiting. The first judgement was right, the second wrong. I was misled by the completely different style in which Yeltsin reaches his decisions. He does not proceed by reason like his predecessor. On the contrary, he likes to appear absolute and authoritarian. He speaks with huge emphasis as if his judgements are immovable, but all the time his gift of political intuition is at work. He is strongly influenced, even as he bangs the table with some absolute pronouncement, by the atmosphere around him and by the way in which he is treated. These intuitions can lead him to shift from one position to another, far removed from the first, but announced with equal force and determination. Yeltsin is not an idealist, but a leader constantly casting around to find solid ground of reality on which he can lead Russia out of the morass in which he found her. He abandoned dictatorship and the command economy, and he presided over the dissolution of the Soviet Union – not because he thought any of these things were wrong in themselves, but because his political instinct showed him that they no longer provided any solid ground on which Russia could stand.

Above *The Congress of Vienna 1814–1815. Restraint in victory kept the old order going.* The Hulton Getty Picture Collection Limited

Below *Victory is no longer enough. Napoleon retreats at the Battle of Waterloo in June 1815.* The Hulton Getty Picture Collection Limited

Benjamin Disraeli (1804–1881) (right) with Bismarck at the Congress of Berlin in 1878. The Great Powers met to tackle the Balkan question, vital to the balance of power, following the Russo-Turkish War 1877–1878. Peace was secured for another thirty years but not, as we know, for ever. The Hulton Getty Picture Collection Limited

Austrian Foreign Minister Prince Clemens von Metternich (1773–1859), the high priest of conservative diplomacy and main architect of the Vienna Settlement. The Hulton Getty Picture Collection Limited

Viscount Castlereagh (1769–1822). As Foreign Secretary he understood and worked well with his continental colleagues, but drew back from a common European foreign policy. The Hulton Getty Picture Collection Limited

Prince Otto von Bismarck (1815–1898), Chancellor and unifier of Germany. He made the mistake of creating a system of alliances which only his own ruthless subtlety could sustain. The Hulton Getty Picture Collection Limited

Kaiser Wilhelm II (1859–1941). In dismissing Bismarck in 1890 he dropped the pilot. By antagonising both Russia and Britain he sank the boat. The Hulton Getty Picture Collection Limited

Below *Archduke Franz Ferdinand (1863–1914) shortly before he and his wife were assassinated in Sarajevo on 28 June 1914. The event lit the five-week fuse which detonated the Great War.* The Hulton Getty Picture Collection Limited

Captain Douglas Hurd of the Seventh Battalion of the Middlesex Regiment, killed in the Battle of the Somme at the age of twenty-one. Lord Hurd

Czar Nicholas II (1868–1918) in military uniform; the young Czarevich was also often dressed in uniform to inspire patriotic fervour. Camera Press Ltd

Woodrow Wilson (1856–1924), the American president who led a crusade for peace with justice until his lance broke in his hand. Camera Press Ltd

Below *Peace negotiations at Versailles. The peace was signed in the Hall of Mirrors. It imposed humiliation on Germany without guaranteeing security for her neighbours, particularly France.* Popperfoto

Lloyd George (1863–1945) with Lord Derby (right) in Paris, 1919. In public Lloyd George spoke of hanging the Kaiser and squeezing Germany until the pips squeaked; privately he would have preferred a more reasonable settlement. The Hulton Getty Picture Collection Limited

Hitler with Mussolini. They neither liked nor trusted each other, but their ambitions held them together while they destroyed the peace, Europe and themselves. Camera Press Ltd

Above *Neville Chamberlain (1869–1940) returns from Munich with an assurance of 'peace in our time'. He was determined to avoid conflict: 'In war, whichever side may call itself the victor, there are no winners, but all are losers.'* Camera Press Ltd

Below *The Potsdam Conference, July 1945: Attlee, Truman and Stalin (L–R) discuss the disarming and occupation of Germany. This time the German problem was less important than their own divisions.* Camera Press Ltd

CHAPTER FOUR

THE GULF WAR AND BOSNIA

Previous page *Downtown Sarajevo in 1992. A Bosnian Special Forces soldier returns fire as he and a group of civilians are targeted by Serb snipers.* Popperfoto

On 2 August 1990 Saddam Hussein, President of Iraq, sent his troops into Kuwait and destroyed its independence in one day. On 27 February 1991 those troops were finally expelled from Kuwait and the war of liberation ended. The Gulf War was (at this time of writing) the last occasion when without disguise or ambiguity one sovereign state committed aggression against another. The aggression was reversed and the aggressor punished by a coalition of willing countries acting with the authority of the UN.

Can the particular be held to prove the general? Does the Gulf War mean that the international community has at last gained the will and the wisdom to rally decisively to the defence of any attacked state? Can that (in the past most frequent) cause of international violence now be eliminated?

Obviously this would be a rash boast. Suppose a second war between Iran and Iraq, a fourth war between Israel and some of her Arab neighbours, a second war between Armenia and Azerbaijan. Many other examples are conceivable. No doubt the larger powers, a regional organisation and the Security Council would bestir themselves in most or all such cases to prevent the fighting, to stop it once it started, to clear up after it was over. But no one could be sure that these efforts would be carried to the dramatic level of Desert Storm, with large numbers of troops and aircraft put at risk because of a total determination that, whatever the cost, the aggression must be reversed.

It is sometimes argued that this total determination was the result not of principle but of oil. Kuwait, according to this argument, would have been left to its fate if it had not possessed 10 per cent of the world's oil reserves. To my surprise something of this thought entered the UN Secretary-General's reply to my question during our talk on the subject. Critics of Western policy argued heatedly three years later that the West would have been resolute in suppressing the Bosnian Serbs if Bosnia had been rich in oil on which the West and its allies depended.

It is easy, though often wrong, to be cynical. The parallel with Bosnia will not wash. As I will argue later, the source of that crisis was not foreign aggression but the unwillingness or inability of the different communities inside Bosnia to live together. Nor does the argument about Kuwaiti oil carry the weight put on it. If the West had been solely concerned with oil it would have concentrated on the oil supply. It would have settled terms quickly with Saddam Hussein, allowed him to keep Kuwait, bought the oil and confined itself to protecting Saudi Arabia and the other Gulf States. There would have been no blazing oil fields, no interruptions of supply, none of the risk to the world economy implicit in Desert Storm. Oil cannot be an adequate explanation for the remarkable display of international firmness.

It would be wrong to push the denial too far. I cannot remember during the late summer, autumn and winter of 1990 that oil was ever put forward as a clinching argument for the effort that the British Government decided to make alongside its allies. From my first immediate telephone conversations from the Foreign Office with Margaret Thatcher in Colorado through her discussions there with President Bush, through the long sequence of allied and UN consultation, the emphasis was on resisting and reversing aggression. But it made a difference that Kuwait was central, important and well known to Britain and many Britons. Its rape was dramatic and highly visible on television. Saddam Hussein hardly made any attempt to throw dust into the eyes of the world. His legal claim on Kuwait was empty and his grievances against Kuwait negligible. His perfunctory effort to find Kuwaiti quislings petered out after a few days. His behaviour, part unctuous part threatening, towards the Western hostages held in Iraq repelled public opinion in the outside world which he was presumably trying to impress. The masochistic part of the Western press liked to portray him as a master of propaganda and subtle tactics, compared to the divided fumblings of their own governments. The reverse was true. Rarely has an aggressor been so ineffective in disguising or excusing his crime, or so generous in providing his enemies with the right arguments to defeat him. We may be faced in the future with more skilful aggressors operating in less clear-cut circumstances and less visible parts of the world.

Nevertheless the rapid mobilisation and then the durability of the coalition which reversed the aggression must stand as a hopeful sign for the future. Because the requirements for the coalition of the willing in the Gulf War may become relevant again, they are worth brief analysis. Resolution comes first, was indispensable and needs no explanation. George Bush proved himself a resolute leader. In the early days Margaret Thatcher showed again a clear-sighted resolution that impressed but in her case did not surprise the world. John Major sustained that resolution during the difficult decisions which followed within weeks of his arrival at 10 Downing Street. Among the allies I recall in particular the steadfastness of the Saudi leaders. They were shocked and shaken by what had happened but showed no inclination to respond by casting around for subtle compromise.

The second requirement was legitimacy. To sustain the effort it was necessary to show the world that this was more than a trial of brute strength between two forces that were morally and legally equivalent. There was a good deal of argument about the best means of ensuring legitimacy. Article 51 of the UN Charter provides an absolute right of self defence. International lawyers argued convincingly that this right extended to allies trying to rescue Kuwait as well as to Kuwait itself. But the American Secretary of State, James Baker, argued with my strong support that this was not enough. In our view we needed specific authorisation of our effort by the Security Council. There were hazards in this course. There was the danger of Russian or Chinese vetoes. More subtle was the danger of fudged and obscure wording in a Security Council resolution which might prevent our commanders in the field from doing what was necessary. We managed through firm diplomacy in New York and in capitals to avoid these dangers. The specific approval of the Security Council was a necessary condition of Allied success.

Third came persuasion. Partly this was a matter of getting

up early in the morning to state and restate to the point of tedium day after day to our own public opinion what we were doing and what was at stake. In Britain this included taking the Labour Party into our confidence. The Labour leadership gave us the general support that we sought, but were naturally vigilant for any slips or contradictions in what we did and said. President Bush had the hardest task. He had to use arguments of idealism and realism alike to convert a reluctant Congress and a sometimes hostile media to a policy that he believes enjoyed throughout the support of most Americans. But persuasion also included work on the doubting states. Russia and China were the most important because of their permanent membership of the Security Council and of their wider strength. But there were also doubting or hostile states nearer the crisis – namely Jordan, Yemen and the PLO. Much effort was required to prevent the angry rift between them and their fellow Arabs from getting out of hand.

The final need was consistency. The coalition of the willing (with its penumbra of doubting but acquiescent countries) was formed and sustained for a particular purpose, namely the rescue of Kuwait. More than once Margaret Thatcher insisted to me in the summer of 1990 that this limited objective should not be extended. Once the Iraqi army was routed in Kuwait in the following February it would have been feasible militarily to press on to Baghdad. No doubt after some days and further casualties we would have been able to overthrow the Government of Saddam Hussein. We would then have had to install a different Iraqi Government and sustain it indefinitely, probably with British and American troops.

By coincidence I was in the White House on the morning of 27 February 1991 when the President and his advisers came to the conclusion that the victory was complete and the war should end at once. In these informal discussions there was no suggestion that the objective of Desert Storm could or should at that last minute be changed. I do not believe that in the formal Cabinet meeting which followed later that day in Washington, or in the exchanges that evening between the President and Allied leaders, anyone proposed pressing on to Baghdad. Nobody wanted to sustain Saddam Hussein in power or believed that he could be transformed in adversity into a trustworthy character. But it was evident to all that the work to which we had put our hands was complete. In his interview with me in May 1997 George Bush explained robustly, as John Major had often done, that the coalition of the willing would have unravelled quickly if its legitimacy had been destroyed and its hold on public opinion undermined by a sudden change of direction.

So the Gulf War achieved its defined and limited purpose. The world as a whole would feel happier and safer if it had also led to a change of Government in Baghdad. As I write Saddam Hussein continues in power. His rule has failed every test except that of self-preservation. Despite his bravado, his people are defeated, poor and isolated. On the day when he is thrust from office the streets will be full of crowds celebrating his overthrow as today from time to time they are mobilised to celebrate his rule. He may well be succeeded by a military man with little zest for democracy, but his successor will not carry the same load of evil as Saddam, with the result that the Arab world and the West will rightly beat a path to his door and look to incorporate Iraq in the international community.

Meanwhile, we have to deal with Saddam Hussein and a regime which has shown ingenious deceit by trying to promote itself to the status of great power by acquiring weapons of mass destruction. The response of the international community has been to impose under the authority of the Security Council a unique system of monitoring and inspection. Saddam Hussein tries to undermine and evade this system, producing occasional crises, for example the one in February 1998. Since economic sanctions are already in place the response of part of the West to these crises has inevitably been at the very top of the scale. The United States and its closest allies have deployed force in the area and threatened to use it if Saddam Hussein continues to undermine the work of the UN. These threats were justified and so far have worked, despite misgivings in Europe and the Arab world. So long as he is in power, Saddam Hussein will try the same game from time to time. He will exploit the quite separate but understandable resentment of Arabs against the United States for failing to hold Israel to her commitments in Palestine. He will hold out half-promises of commercial favours to countries like Russia and France who, until the eleventh hour of a crisis, like to make a show of opposition to American leadership. He will try to shift the blame for the sufferings of the Iraqi people away from himself on to the UN and the Anglo-Saxon in particular.

In response to this barrage of argument the United States has to be more skilful in keeping together the 'coalition of the willing' which George Bush formed in 1990–1991. One of the main threats to peace in the next century is the spread of nuclear, biological and chemical weapons. Iraq is at present the main illustration of that threat. This is a subject on which it is not safe to be weary. The effort to contain, then eliminate, the threat has to succeed.

In the last few years much of the argument about idealism and realism in the making of foreign policy has taken the war in

Bosnia as a text – though a text from which widely differing sermons are preached. In 1998 we are in an intermediate stage. The immediate passionate books have been written. Settled verdicts will not be with us for some time yet. The Bosnian War (like the Spanish Civil War in the 1930s) packs an exceptional charge of emotion. It will continue to attract controversy long after those who fought and made peace have disappeared. In this no-man's land between instant comment and history I do not want to analyse in detail the course of British, Western or UN policy during the war. There may come a time for that. We do not yet know whether the Dayton Agreement of autumn 1995 amounted to a peace or an armistice. The bandages are still in place; it is not clear whether under them the patient's wounds have begun to heal. But even without that fundamental uncertainty about the future of Bosnia, indeed the whole of ex-Yugoslavia, another underlying reason restrains comment. People write most easily about enterprises that they believe to have been wholly triumphant or wholly disastrous. The words flow most readily when the author wishes either to boast or to denounce. Neither mood (it seems to me) begins to fit the Western effort in Bosnia. We made a sustained attempt to deal with an appalling tragedy, and it was not good enough. The story is encrusted with myths that should one day be scraped away. But for the purpose of this book it will be enough to look briefly, and I hope soberly, at the balance that was struck between idealism and realism and to study some of the means used to see if they hold future lessons in the search for peace.

First a word of comparison with the Gulf War which came immediately before it. On any calculation of national interest, the Gulf War was more important for Britain than Bosnia. We deployed more men in the Gulf; we lost more men. The whole enterprise was a greater one so far as Britain was concerned. Yet in my memory the decisions we took as a War Cabinet under two Prime Ministers, Margaret Thatcher and John Major, in 1990 and 1991 as regards the Gulf were smoother and more straightforward than those we took about Bosnia. They were less controversial, not in the sense that they were less important, or that less hung on them, because probably more did. But they were less controversial between the colleagues around the Cabinet table, in the House of Commons, and among the Allies. In the Gulf there was a clear line of United States leadership. This did not mean that we all did what the US wanted, but the US was clearly the leader of the coalition. The whole range of decisions seemed to be straightforward. One decision followed logically on from another. The aggressor committed the aggression and seized Kuwait in a day; a coalition quite rapidly formed to say that was unacceptable. The aggressor was asked to remove himself; he did not do so. Sanctions were applied; he was asked again to remove himself; he stayed. Forces were deployed; he was again asked to remove himself. He stayed; he was bombed. He remained, and eventually he was thrown out by an enterprise on land. There was a steady sequence of events. A coalition was formed and had to be maintained. One read constantly in the better-informed newspapers that the coalition was about to dissolve, but it never did. We held it together against the odds. The exercise ended with the success of the purpose for which it had been devised, the liquidation of the aggression. I look back on that as a relatively straightforward exercise, a relatively straightforward series of crucially important decisions.

By contrast Bosnia was intellectually and ethically tangled. There was no clear leader of the effort, no master plan, no master organisation. Each country formed a view and then tried to work with others. We tried not to be entirely pragmatic. In London, in Brussels, in Washington we were forever trying to cut through the tangle by applying tests of principle. There are different possible tests of principle to which the realist and the idealist will give different weights. By the test of narrow national interest Bosnia could not rate high for the British. No one sitting down calmly in Whitehall to assess where in Britain's interests we should deploy British troops or focus British economic aid would have picked on Bosnia as a recipient. There was a British interest in preventing a general Balkan war, a substantial quarrel between the West and Yeltsin's reforming Russia, or a serious rift within NATO or within the EU. All these were important negative objectives for the realist. We had to spend a good deal of time on them at different stages. But they were consequent, not central to Bosnia itself. One set of critics often reminded us of Bismarck's reported phrase that the Balkans were not worth the bones of a single Pomeranian grenadier. The instinct of the realist was to stay out.

The second test was ethical. The aim of the idealists was peace with justice. They do not necessarily go together, as the later argument over war criminals has shown. You can have peace without justice, though hardly justice without peace. But from 1992 to 1995 that would have seemed a quibble, since the former Yugoslavia suffered from an abundance of both war and injustice. There was little difficulty in Britain or the West about the principle of military intervention to help secure peace with justice. The British Cabinet does not usually spend much time mulling over disputes of doctrine. Not many of my colleagues would have pointed out that the fighting was being done by Bosnians in Bosnia and that the UN Charter forbade intervention in the internal affairs of a member state. If the firm and rapid use of military force would have stopped the fighting (let alone brought peace with justice) we would have agreed it. Casualties would have been accepted if a quick and favourable outcome could have been assured. But professional advice allied to common sense repeatedly indicated that this was a hallucination.

The third test to be applied in a democracy is public opinion. Realists and idealists have to concur on this. Public opinion cannot lead, neither can it be ignored. A major military enterprise could not be undertaken by Britain against the settled weight of British public opinion. Although public opinion could not force a government to undertake an enterprise against its better judgement, it can powerfully influence that judgement. On Bosnia no such influence was exerted. There was shock and anger at the atrocities reported on the television screen. Groups among the public and individuals in the media strongly advocated particular steps to help the underdog, namely the Bosnian Muslims. It seemed possible that the general indignation and the individual advocacy of particular measures might fuse into a powerful pressure for intervention. It never happened. The fuse spluttered but the explosive was never detonated. The main Opposition Party remained quiescent. In the Cabinet and in Parliament the general mood restrained rather than encouraged the Government. Indeed from time to time the ministers in daily charge of policy found difficulty in obtaining the necessary minimum of consent from their own colleagues for forward steps that we judged necessary.

Other Western governments applied the same three tests to their policies – the tests of national interest, of peace with justice, of public opinion. They arrived at somewhat differing conclusions, but the differences were of degree. No one favoured standing aside from Bosnia completely. No one was ready to stop the killing by taking the country over and imposing a just solution. As usual in such cases, neither the option of doing nothing nor the option of doing everything turned out to be practicable. When it came to the point everyone favoured limited intervention. Judgements varied from time to time and from country to country as to the best combination of means. The United States faced a familiar dilemma. More than most European countries (but like Germany) it tended to see the conflict in terms of good (Muslim and sometimes Croats) against evil (Serbs and sometimes Croats). More than most European countries (but again like Germany) it disliked the idea of involving its own troops, and above all of risking casualties. Neither the Bush nor the Clinton administrations, before 1995, sustained a coherent Bosnia policy. Their interest ebbed and flowed. They tended to favour methods that appeared forthright and involved the least risk. The American media were quick to criticise others who had ventured more than the US in Bosnia, but achieved scant success. They were comforted in this stance by the foolishness of some European politicians who at the outset indicated that Europe could tackle the problem without the United States.

The European Union thought and talked endlessly about Bosnia. Unwisely we allowed it to be assumed that the success of our own Union could be tested by our ability to resolve this war outside our own borders. One of the encrusting myths is that the European Union was paralysed by division. Rather we were united in frustration. There were arguments about tactics and timing, for example in the recognition of Croatia and Slovenia, but no fundamental disagreement. The limited intervention that we undertook was not a compromise between those who wanted to do everything and those who wanted to do nothing, since no government held either position. The continuous diplomatic efforts through Lord Carrington, David Owen, the Contact Group, the London Conferences, the substantial economic aid, and the preponderant European troop contributions to the UN force were painfully worked out to influence events for the better. The mastery of events eluded us. It remained in the hands of those who were fighting. We saw no acceptable means of wresting it from them.

The other substantial outside power was, or could have been, Russia. Russian opinion favoured the Serbs but there too the lit fuse never reached the explosive. There was no outburst of popular feeling. The Russians were not particularly effective either in helping or in restraining the Serbs. Like the Europeans they made an effort, but their frustration was as great as ours. Towards the end they gave the impression that their central aim was procedural. It was essential to them that Moscow should be fully informed and consulted. What was decided was less important.

No one, whether idealist or realist, American, European or Russian can take pleasure in their performance during this story. That is different from allocating to any of them primary guilt. The repeated miscalculation of the leaders of all three Bosnian communities were accompanied by the atrocities committed mainly by Bosnian Serbs and Bosnian Croats. Responsibility for disaster rests with those who actually bring it about, not with others who might conceivably by acting differently have deterred them or lessened the consequences.

Nevertheless it must be right to look at the different methods used by the international community in Bosnia to draw lessons for the future from their relative success or failure.

Everyone is in favour of preventive diplomacy, which carries little cost or risk. It is obviously sensible to forestall if possible either a conflict between states or a civil war. This requires foresight. It also requires the consent of those who are in control of a territory at the onset of danger. If those in charge of Yugoslavia immediately after Tito's death in 1980 had foreseen the destruction that would follow, they might conceivably have agreed to a diplomatic settlement with terms similar to those eventually agreed at Dayton in 1995 for Croatia and Bosnia. But it is an absurd hypothesis. The outside world could not have put forward such a proposal, nor would the Yugoslav authorities have dreamed of considering it. The need for forceful preventive diplomacy usually becomes apparent after the best moment for it has gone. Nevertheless the stakes are so high that past disappointments cannot be conclusive. The Secretary-General of the UN and the heads of regional organisations should be bolder than in the past to draw attention to looming troubles within as well as between states and should be encouraged and equipped to send people of high quality to wrestle with them.

Much has been written about the worth of international sanctions, and the usual verdict is sceptical. The sanctions applied by the Security Council against the Serb-led Government of the Federal Republic of Yugoslavia were extraordinarily difficult to enforce, at sea, by land and on the Danube. The neighbour states complained bitterly and understandably about the loss to their own economies. Evasion was widespread. Smuggling became an even more lucrative profession than is usual in the Balkans. Nevertheless the main aim of the international community was achieved. President Milosevic changed policy under the pressure of sanctions, deserted the Bosnian Serb allies whom he had encouraged to war, tried to compel them into the Vance Owen plan, and eventually succeeded in driving them to accept Dayton. The gradual impoverishment and isolation of his country induced him to abandon, at least for the time being, the thrust for a greater Serbia. That change of heart was one of the essential pressures which led to the winding down of the war. Alas, it proved temporary.

The aspect of sanctions that caused most difficulty was the arms embargo. It seemed at the outset both idealism and realism to deny weapons to the combatants in a war that the international community wished to end. But harsh argument flared up between those who saw the fighting as essentially the result of aggression (in which case the attacked party was entitled to the means of self-defence) or essentially a civil war (in which case the argument for the arms embargo held). The arms embargo was supported until the end of the war by the European Union, the majority of the UN Security Council, and the leadership of the three British political parties. When those who opposed the arms embargo, notably the US Administration and the Bosnian Government, had to choose between ending the arms embargo and continuing the UN force in Bosnia they chose the latter. The dilemma was eased towards the end of the war by the surreptitious supply of weapons to the Croats and Muslims. The only moral which can safely be drawn is the need for more effective staff work and the pooling of intelligence among those who have to take international decisions. Shared intelligence will not guarantee agreed decisions, but it helps to remove some of the obstacles.

The intervention of UN troops in Bosnia saved thousands of lives, and that was its justification. The UN force often damped down but could not extinguish the conflict. As a result it has become fashionable, particularly in American military circles, to argue that if there is to be any military intervention in such cases in the future it must be absolute, with a clear objective, a clear timescale and probably an identified enemy. That is desirable, but I do not believe things will always work out that way. The international community is likely from time to time to plump again for limited intervention with objectives that shift with time.

But there were two defects in the Bosnian intervention so glaring that they are unlikely to be repeated. First, the ground effort was in the hands of one organisation and the air effort in the hands of another. The UN and NATO have different membership, different rules, different characteristics. In military operations it is not unusual to have to strike a balance between what you can achieve by air strikes and the safety of your troops on the ground. But usually this balance is worked out quickly and privately under a single command. In Bosnia it was argued through in semi-public between two different commands. The arrangement by which every air strike had to be agreed by both NATO and the UN was called the 'dual key'. They fumbled over the dual key and often dropped it. As a result the usefulness of air strikes was not fully exploited until 1995. The distribution of tasks in Bosnia is much more workman-like now.

Second, and in the public's perception even more damaging, was the collapse of the safe areas. The moral here is that idealistic concepts are particularly risky in military operations. It was defensible to want to add the idea of defined safe areas to the existing limited intervention. Two conditions were necessary, which were never achieved – the demilitarisation of the areas so that they would not be used as protected bases for offensive action against the Serbs, and large numbers of extra men in UN blue helmets. The Secretary-General appealed for such reinforcements but did not receive them. The policy should not have been proclaimed unless both conditions were within reach of fulfilment. As it was, the UN force was stretched into dispositions that made no military sense. The British were in danger in one safe area (Gorazde) and the Dutch faced humiliation in another (Srebrenica). Although the Bosnian Government knew the real situation, its citizens and the world as a whole did not. The concept of safe areas was thus constantly exposed as a mockery. Democratic politicians are often tempted to announce their aims as if they were achievements, but more often than not this is a disaster.

These mistakes on the part of the international community should not obscure the fundamental lesson of Bosnia. When Yugoslavia broke up the Serbs rejected the idea that the boundaries of the different Yugoslav republics, as drawn by Tito, should be accepted as the boundaries of new nation states. They did this because it would mean that large numbers of Serbs would have to live outside Serbia, as minorities in Croatia and Bosnia. They went to war for self-determination. Woodrow Wilson would have understood their aim while being appalled by their methods. But you cannot divide South-Eastern Europe simply on the basis of self-determination. Even ruthless ethnic cleansing fails to achieve this. Communities live in a mixed-up tangle of towns and villages; the mosaic is the mosaic is the mosaic. That is why Yugoslavia came into being in 1919 and why the Dayton Agreement provided for a multi-ethnic Croatia and a multi-ethnic Bosnia. But they in turn will depend on the willingness of neighbours to live side by side in peace, resisting the calls to hate and fear each other. I never believed that the wars in Yugoslavia were inevitable, any more than sectarian strife in Northern Ireland is inevitable. Leaders unforgivably conjured up hatred from the past, which for a time overwhelmed the needs of the present.

Not many miles from the flames of the war in Bosnia and Croatia were stacked other bonfires of combustible material, waiting to blaze up if the wind blew in their direction – Macedonia, Montenegro, Volvodjna. But the most dangerous was Kosovo, the south-western segment of Serbia, nine-tenths of whose inhabitants are now Albanian. To this problem, as to many in international affairs (Cyprus is another example), the right answer is clear enough provided you stand far enough away from it. But as you approach, the smoke of the fire obscures vision and what seemed clear turns out to be impossible. Kosovo ought to be given back the autonomy within Serbia which Milosevic took from them. But this answer, which we repeatedly urged on Milosevic during the Bosnian War, was rejected by him as unthinkable. The battlefield (1389) and the monasteries of Kosovo were part of the essence of Serbia, and there was nothing more to be said.

The common-sense solution is also now rejected by most of the Albanian majority in Kosovo. When the Kosovan bonfire began to crackle and burn in the spring of 1998, American and British leaders promised that they had learned from the experience of Bosnia and would handle this matter much more quickly. They were quite right in this ambition, but mistaken if they felt that they had been vouchsafed some helpful revelation of how to achieve it. Once again it was equally unacceptable to do nothing or to do everything. Once again, while Albanians and Serbs killed each other, the powers slowly experimented with a mix of familiar techniques of limited intervention: preventive diplomacy, the amber, red, green lights of sanctions, air strikes, civilian monitors, possible military deployment.

At least this time Americans and Europeans worked closely together from the outset, and the Russians, though reluctant, were involved through the inherited machinery of the contact group. Milosevic has turned his back again on the prospect which he seemed earlier to embrace at Dayton, that Serbia might change policy and belatedly join the process which is sweeping his neighbours into the European structures of security and prosperity. By repressing Kosovo and indeed Montenegro, Serbia is contracting out of Europe's hopeful future. She is entitled to her myths and dreams but cannot live on them. Both communities in Ireland have now come to understand this. One day Milosevic or his successor will do the same.

The parallels with Ireland are worth a closer glance. During the years of turmoil in Bosnia I was often reminded of a big sheet which used to hang in my office in Stormont Castle when I was Secretary of State for Northern Ireland in 1984–1985. It was a street plan of the city of Belfast mapped out in a confusion of orange and green. It looked like one of those modern paintings which consist of two pots of paint thrown at a canvas. Protestant and Catholic districts were not neatly separated but intermingled, district by district, street by street. The same was true of the border counties of Down, Armagh, Fermanagh, Tyrone and Londonderry. No redrawing of the map would produce a neat line combining geography and politics, with each community living in tribal purity within its own boundaries. That is why the Good Friday Agreement at Stormont in 1998, like the Dayton Agreement of 1995 on Bosnia, represents a desperate effort, strongly urged from outside, to create a political structure within which the communities can live at peace within changing boundaries. Stormont, like Dayton, contains little innovation; it reassembles fragments of past agreements which at the time seemed for a moment to prosper but then disintegrated. Neither agreement marks the end of conflict. There may never be a moment when we can say with conviction: 'Thank God that conflict is over; no one will ever be killed there again for political reasons.' We can say that now of Alsace-Lorraine; maybe our grandchildren will be able to say it of Bosnia and Northern Ireland. But time works slowly, and its healing power is uncertain. Meanwhile, the Irish problem is like a steeplechase without a finishing post. You have to take the fences to survive and progress, but they seem to stretch endlessly into the distance.

Thanks in particular to the energy and courage of Tony Blair and the Unionist leader David Trimble, the Stormont Agreement was a huge fence bravely jumped. The Agreement rests on a principle, the principle of consent, which in the past was widely contested. It is not so long since most of those who thought and cared about Irish politics believed that Irish unity must be the principle underlying any settlement; that only the undoing of partition and the abolition of the border would secure an end to troubles. This was the view of the Americans, of all parties in the Irish Republic, of the nationalist minority in the North, and of the British Labour Party. Only the Unionists in the North and the British Conservatives argued that the democratic consent of the majority in the North was crucial. Neither of these was persuasive because the Unionist record on democracy in the North was distinctly dodgy. Gradually over the years the argument swung round, thanks largely to the ending of discrimination in the North under direct rule from Britain, and to the work of Tony Blair's predecessors, Ted Heath, Margaret Thatcher and John Major. Each of these achieved an agreement which turned out temporary and imperfect, but which edged the argument forward towards the acceptance of consent. The Americans, Fine Gael, later Fianna Fail, and the British Labour Party came round over the years. Only Sinn Fein are still hesitant over the proposition that the constitutional future of Northern Ireland must always depend on the wishes of the majority, who in turn must guarantee the equitable rights of the minority and accept a limited role for the Republic in the forming of a number of all-Ireland bodies.

It is perverse against this background that the main dissent from the Stormont Agreement came from the Unionist camp, even though they had won the main argument. Perverse, but understandable. The protest was not so much against the proposed institutions but against the premature release of terrorist murderers and the failure to guarantee that their weapons would be destroyed. These shortcomings in the Agreement underscored the ambivalence of the IRA's conversion to democracy by appearing to leave them the resources to return to the bullet should they dislike the results of the ballot box. But the emphatic majority in the referendum in the North were prepared to take that risk.

The reasons for this acceptance have a significance which reaches beyond Ireland. How was Ian Paisley able to destroy the Sunningdale Agreement in 1974 but unable to destroy the Stormont Agreement in 1998? Increased prosperity north and south of the border must be part of the answer. More and more people concern themselves with jobs, careers, qualifications, less and less with the traditional enmities of the two communities. In the past too many in Northern Ireland have turned their backs on politics and constructed lives outside the political process. As a result politics in the Province failed to adapt, and became stuck in the old grooves. By 1998 sufficient voters were ready to come back into politics and insist that the future have priority over the past. It remains to be seen whether this admirable impetus will persist through the long drawn-out processes of carrying through the Agreement for which that majority voted.

So the Agreement was based on acceptance of self-determination within a Province sliced away seventy-six years earlier from the rest of Ireland. But as Woodrow Wilson and the peace makers after 1918 discovered, self-determination does not work in all cases. It is a technique rather than an overriding principle. Applied in the 1860s it would have meant the partition of the United States. Applied in the 1930s it meant the integration of the Sudeten Germans with Hitler's Reich and the end of Czechoslovakia. What really counted at Stormont was not the content of the Agreement but the fact that it was achieved. It was contrived with much difficulty by the force of reconciliation and only continued reconciliation can make it work. The same is true in Bosnia, and indeed in South Africa. The circumstances of these three enduring dramas are quite different, but in each case exhaustion, allied to pressures and encouragement from outside, created an impetus towards reconciliation which in turn produced an agreement. We cannot tell yet whether the impetus to reconciliation will be strong enough to sustain and develop those agreements decade by decade until the destructive bitterness of the past shrinks into a memory. The real preventive diplomacy is not mainly between governments and politicians but between lawyers and historians, tribe and tribe, the church on one side of a village street and the rival church or mosque on the other.

CHAPTER FIVE

INTERLUDE

Thursday 10 October 1996, Tbilisi, Georgia

We arrived at 4.30 a.m. from Istanbul and were met by two young men on behalf of the Georgian Government. George seemed to have been set the task of delaying our entry into his country for as long as possible; Alexander, brisk and chirpy, steered us around the bureaucratic obstacles and inspections organised by George. Georgia is likewise balanced between the old and the new. I am not quite sure how the interview with Edward Shevardnadze will go tomorrow. In the five years since I knew him well he has passed from being Soviet Foreign Minister to President of his own country. It has been a stormy passage, accompanied by much violence and at least one attempt on his life. His response to my letter was very welcoming, but I am not sure whether he will want to talk about the wide foreign policy themes which dominate our programme, or whether he will insist on a detailed discussion of his own local problems. Probably a bit of both.

Managed to write 2,000 words of my novel on the plane, as well as to finish *The Suitable Boy*. Next comes the *Heart of Midlothian*, because I can't remember it, and some time ago at Eton the Headmaster, Eric Anderson, told me it was the easiest of Scott's novels for the sceptic.

Friday 11 October 1996

An excellent day, such as a travelling Foreign Secretary can never manage because he is pinned into set meetings in the capital. Breakfast in this Austrian-run hotel with the French Foreign Minister, Hervé de Charette. I eat breakfast while he smokes. He is friendly but gloomy about the prospect of Europe ever coming together on foreign policy. I fear that we and the French have missed an opportunity. If ten or fifteen years ago we had come together on five or six of the main foreign policy issues we could have carried the Germans and then the other countries and become by now a valid partner of the Americans. But we and the French pile up in our own minds reservations about each other which get in the way of effective co-operation even when, as often, our ideas and interests more or less coincide. It was a pleasure to overcome for the time being these reservations and work closely on Bosnia with Hervé's predecessor, Alain Juppé. Seen close to, the French are effective defenders of their own essential interests, and at heart no enemy of ours, despite traditional snarlings.

Proceed with the BBC team to Stalin's birthplace, Gori. The Georgian authorities offered it and producer Matthew Barrett was keen to accept. This is Soviet Union old-style, even though it is now planted in the heart of independent Georgia. In the town square is a huge statue of Stalin, said to be the only one remaining in the former Soviet Union. When the troops arrived with instructions from Moscow to demolish the statue, the townspeople simply stood in the square to protect it, and it was spared. The birthplace is a tiny shoemaker's cottage, encased in a preposterous Soviet pillared building. Behind, a massive museum with plenty of photographs recording the blossoming of the young German seminarist into the suspicious and bloodthirsty dictator. There is really nothing to be said in posthumous defence of either Hitler or Stalin. Both were thoroughly destructive and appeared to have no honourable motives. Stalin was more successful in concealing his cruelties. Even so, it is surprising that he deceived Roosevelt so effectively at Yalta. Less surprising that, unlike Hitler, he retained, even among his fiercest critics in Russia, a formidable reputation as the saviour of the country in the Great Patriotic War. If Woodrow Wilson was the thorough-going idealist in this story, then I suppose Bismarck and Stalin were the thorough-going realists. But Bismarck operated within the framework of nineteenth-century civilisation, whereas Stalin made his own framework to suit his own murderous instincts.

Georgia has two civil wars bubbling at the moment, but one of them is relatively quiet, so we are allowed to visit it. There are no frontier posts between Georgia and the province of South Ossetia which, until recently, was in revolt, helped by the North Ossetians across the border in Russia. The houses in the village we visit were solidly built, but one or two are in ruins and just about all of them have bullet holes. The trees are heavy with red apples, and the rolling countryside looks mellow in the mild autumn sunshine. We talk to peasant women who have just returned to houses from which they had fled for several months after being attacked by rebels. We move on to the capital of South Ossetia, Tsinkvali, a quiet mess with many wrecked houses. Russian peace keepers patrol the streets. I talk to a tall, fair young soldier from St Petersburg, who understands English. I ask him whether he feels the Russian army is on a useful mission in South Ossetia. He is about to reply when a colonel intervenes and whisks me off.

Back in Gori we are given an old-fashioned lunch. It is not quite clear who is the host, but many dignitaries are present, including the unbuttoned General Nikolaev, in command of the Russian peace keepers. The BBC team and I are anxious to get back to Tbilisi for our interview with Shevardnadze. We eat a substantial meal and exchange numerous toasts, but I realise just after we get up to go that many more dishes are waiting in the wings. The dignitaries had come expecting to tuck in throughout the afternoon. Georgian wine is abundant and tastes better in Georgia than in Moscow. A country whose main products are apples, wine and brandy should one day be happy.

The interview with Shevardnadze is admirable. He speaks to us for about two hours. He has lost none of his diplomatic caution, but is I think entirely genuine when he speaks of his comradeship with Gorbachev and how they determined together to change the whole course of Soviet foreign policy. The trigger was the hopeless inadequacy of the justifications given to them for the Soviet invasion of Afghanistan. He and Gorbachev were on holiday on the Black Sea when the news came to them from Moscow that the decision had been taken to move into Afghanistan. He said that they both reacted with silent outrage which could not be articulated at the time. He felt that the Afghan War, if one took into account its final results, was more devastating to the Soviet Union than the Vietnam War was to America. The Afghan War, which lasted almost eleven years, helped to waken Soviet society to reality. People began to assess critically the traditions of Soviet foreign policy and political life in general.

I asked him about the two concessions by Gorbachev which, at the time, struck me as amazing – first the ease with which he allowed East Germany, the model Communist state, to collapse, and second how Gorbachev and Shevardnadze agreed to the unification of Germany, even accepting that the unified Germany should be a full member of NATO. Shevardnadze recalled these decisions calmly as part of the crisis of the socialist system. Certainly he and Gorbachev knew that they were swimming against the tide of Russian opinion. They prevailed because they genuinely believed in the changes which were necessary and also because, as General Secretary of the Communist Party of the Soviet Union, Gorbachev had power of which any emperor would be envious. Had Gorbachev not possessed that power, the opposition would have crushed him and deprived them of any chance to realise their ideas.

These were, of course, topics which he and I had discussed before during the long two-plus-four negotiations on Germany in which we had been partners in 1990 and 1991. Margaret Thatcher had her serious anxieties about German unification and would have liked to impede it if others had been prepared to join her. So these had been difficult discussions for me as well as for Shevardnadze, which was perhaps why we both remembered them so well. But his difficulties had been immensely greater. He and Gorbachev were being accused of throwing away the objectives for which the Soviet Union had fought and suffered during the Great

Patriotic War. This conversation five years later persuaded me of something of which I had not been certain: that he and Gorbachev were not simply responding to pressures from the West and from their former satellites. They were following a considered line based on principles which they had worked out in private together during the frustrations of the Afghan War.

In the evening President Shevardnadze gave us a banquet in the guest house built for the master of Soviet terror, Beria. The security surrounding him was formidable. At no time did he harp upon the difficulties being faced by Georgia. He did, however, often repeat that the principles of the new world order had to apply to all countries and that Georgia, even though distant from the West, was entitled to the same kind of help in its difficulties as any other country.

Saturday 12 October 1997

Before we left Tbilisi there was time to look around in the company of the newly arrived British Ambassador, Stephen Nash. Tbilisi has its share of Soviet monstrosities but has preserved, despite the bullet holes, traditional streets – elegant houses with balconies of iron and wood, an occasional caravanserai, where the travellers slept above in the upper galleries of the courtyard, and their beasts below. A learned lady escorted us through three of the many churches, crowded with worshippers. Stephen Nash took me somewhat tentatively to the dilapidated but elegant town house in which he hopes to establish the British Embassy. It stands on a bluff on the river, opposite the old town. It seemed to me just right. Would the Foreign Office be able to find the money? Since the total budget is being cut, opening in Georgia means cutting elsewhere. Georgia is not rich and will not be prosperous at least until it begins to benefit from the proposed pipeline leading from the oil fields round the Caspian to the Black Sea. But are we to be absent from a new and friendly country which certainly has strategic importance and will probably provide its share of the world's problems and sufferings? If we intend to retain anything like a worldwide foreign policy then we need to be among those present. It is not by accident that the French Foreign Minister is paying a visit.

We leave with some regret, but also with a reminder that the twists of history have contradictory effects on individuals. Georgia is free again, no longer ruled from Moscow. The Soviet Union has disappeared. But for some this is a sadness. I mentioned earlier my friendly young security escort, Alexander. It emerges that he was a promising young tennis player in Soviet times. He travelled about the Communist world at the expense of the Government. He had excellent teachers, equipment and facilities. After the break-up of the Soviet Union he had to go to work at a holiday resort in Turkey. The pay was good, but he was entirely alone and separated from his family and friends. Now he is back with them, but his job as security guard is negligible compared with his career as a tennis star. He is twenty-one, and after the excitements of his early youth has had to sell his car and rely again on financial help from his father. He wakes up at night worrying about his future. He thinks that I need additional security in England and someone who could teach me tennis.

Saturday 12 October 1996, Vienna

A brief visit to the room in the Foreign Ministry where

modern peace making began. The helpful lady with orange hair could not confirm that Metternich had arranged for five doors to be created so that the representatives of the five main Allies could enter the room simultaneously. Do a piece to camera on the treaty-making accomplished here in 1814. This was pre-American diplomacy, realism at its coolest. The only ideology with which they were concerned was the perverted idealism of the French Revolution, which they were determined to abolish for good. Nothing to do with human rights, nothing to do with disarmament, nothing to do of course with economics or the environment. Just the hard slog of traditional diplomacy. Except that they had two flashes of insight. They treated France generously; and they saw that some sort of concert of Europe was going to be needed to sustain the peace which they were negotiating.

The Austrians pack their tragedies quite close. In the next room is the plaque showing where Chancellor Dollfuss was killed by Nazi supporters in 1934.

We film in Vienna one afternoon only. The BBC team manage to get their gear out of the airport, into a van, to the Balhaus Platz, back to the airport, through all the procedures, and into the plane so that we can reach London by evening. Our cameraman, who perhaps has never had a political thought in his life, remarks, 'Thank God for Europe.' Before the Single Market did away with bureaucratic frontier procedures it would have been impossible for him to film just for one afternoon in Vienna. The documentation and inspections would have made this out of the question. Now he can film in Vienna as easily as in Oxford. Metternich would have seen the point, while no doubt finding the idea of a television programme on foreign policy wholly repulsive.

Monday 11 November 1996, Hamburg

Up at 5.00 a.m. and out into frosty darkness. By BA to the Atlantic Hotel, Hamburg. Walk round the Alster basis, calm and elegant. Two hours with Helmut Schmidt in the hotel. Recall escorting him to Oxford to receive his degree when he was Federal Chancellor sixteen years ago. He is plumper in the face and a little deaf, but mind and tongue sharp and lively as ever. Smokes cigarettes and takes snuff. He is a man of power, expert at relations between states, scornful of the Kaiser but not of Bismarck. Not particularly interested in generalities on human rights, as his comments on both Serbs and Chinese make clear. Untypical of the present quality of political debate in Germany, which in both main parties is befogged with repetition of principles.

Wednesday 13 November 1996, London

It was some time since I had talked to Denis Healey. When he opened the door of his Pimlico flat to let me in I thought we had made a terrible mistake. He was slobbering, his mouth open, his jaw dropped, his eyes vacant. It was hardly possible to hear what he said. For a few seconds it seemed clear that he had had a stroke and lapsed into senility. The joke over, he played his usual rumbustious self. There is no such thing as a defensive Denis Healey. Teasing provocation is his stock-in-trade. He is quite prepared to be inaccurate in order to be outrageous, and remains good company throughout. He provides whisky. We plough through the arguments of the 1930s. It is hard to defend the conduct of Neville Chamberlain, but impossible to justify Labour policy in those years. Denis Healey wisely reverts to attacking the Tories.

Once we get to the post-war years his opinion and mine coincide at almost all points, but he finds this hard to accept and ends up by manufacturing for purposes of argument a conspiracy by the West to keep Saddam Hussein in power. His assertions are 100 per cent confident and 50 per cent accurate.

Wednesday 7 May 1997, New York

Three good interviews today with old friends whom I respect.

It is quite something to have worked continuously either for the United Nations or on United Nations matters since the UN was born fifty years ago. It is even more remarkable that Brian Urquhart looks and sounds exactly the same today as he did when I knew him in New York forty years ago. He has a thoroughly English mind and manner, speaking about matters for which he deeply cares as if they were of small importance, even slightly ridiculous. His analysis of both past and future is deep and competent, but he likes to set it out as a series of anecdotes. We delve again together into the character of Dag Hammarskjöld, whom Brian knew as well as anyone – 'No pond was too messy or too deep for him to jump into.' That was not the reputation with which he started. He was put forward for the Secretary-Generalship by the British and French, who felt that what was needed was a sound European civil servant who would behave like the revered Sir Eric Drummond of the League of Nations, and avoid all the scrapes into which the first Secretary-General, Trygve Lie, had landed the UN. And indeed that was how Dag Hammarskjöld started. But as his self-confidence grew so did his concept of the office which he held. Article 99 of the Charter gives the Secretary-General a vague responsibility for looking into matters which might threaten the peace and reporting on them. Hammarskjöld developed this into a powerful legal and political instrument. In his later years he became something of a high priest, held back only by his own intelligence and integrity. It was an irony that at the time of Suez he felt bound to hold the line against the two great powers which had brought him forward and whom he most respected: Britain and France.

As regards the future, Brian Urquhart felt that member states would soon have to decide whether they really wanted the United Nations to have executive power or simply to be a talking shop. It was no use expecting the UN to intervene effectively in failed states like Somalia if they were not able actually to exercise authority and run things. This conversation strengthened a thought which was drawn to my mind about the need to revive the concept of UN trusteeship.

If Hammarskjöld was a high priest of yesterday, Henry Kissinger is the high priest of foreign affairs today. He is strongly established in his office on Park Avenue, with a covey of ex-Ambassadors associated with him. The quantity and quality of his production continue to be formidable. His master work, *Diplomacy*, is one of the antecedents of our television programme. No one else has set out so clearly the tension between idealism and realism, particularly in the formation of American policy. Kissinger has the reputation of plumping rather hard for realism – 'Most people suppose that I read Metternich by candlelight.' It is true that he argues strongly that idealism, even American idealism, comes to grief if it parts company with reality, as did Woodrow Wilson. But on the other hand he is clear that for the world in general and for the United States in particular, a purely cynical and selfish approach is equally unrealistic.

As well as developing these thoughts we gossip separately about the conundrums of the day. Henry is worried about American policy towards China. There are too many people in the United States trying to turn China into an enemy. Human rights issues should certainly be raised persistently with the Chinese, but in the context of a friendly relationship, not as brickbats to rouse public opinion against China. In general he fears that it will be increasingly difficult for any US Admin-istration to pursue consistent long-range policies if these are criticised by lobbies and focus groups. There may no longer be the settled body of informed opinion which would support a President in riding through these ephemeral pressures.

I remember Dick Holbrooke as a performer rather than a philosopher. His technique of quick, brisk action was just what was needed in the closing stages of the Bosnian War. The combatants, the Russians, the UN, NATO and the Allies were hustled from action to action with the minimum of con-sultation. Such American tactics would not have worked at the outset. By the time Dick Holbrooke appeared on the scene all three Bosnian combatants were exhausted. The Bosnian Serbs no longer believed that they were invincible. The Bosnian Muslims no longer believed that the arms embargo would be lifted so as to give them complete victory. Milosevic no longer backed the Bosnian Serbs. The Bosnian Serbs, by humiliating UNPROFOR, had united Alliance opinion in favour of reinforcing the UN on the ground and using NATO more decisively from the air. Dick Holbrooke brought all these factors together and compelled all concerned into the Dayton Agreement. I had left the Foreign Office several months before Dayton, and we spent some time today hashing over the sequence of events. He was less combative in his memories than he had been in argument at the time. As a practitioner he saw no real conflict between realism and idealism in American policy making, but like Henry Kissinger he worried about relationships with China, in particular in Tibet if the Dalai Lama were to die.

That night finished the third of Pat Barker's trilogy. I had bought The *Ghost Road* at Gatwick and in New York had hurried to Doubleday to buy *Regeneration* and *The Eye in the Door*. It was a mistake to read the three books the wrong way round since the last, *The Ghost Road*, is the strongest. Barker dwells on the conflict which besieged the minds of many who fought in the Great War. On the one hand she puts great emphasis on the brutality and the suffering. Siegfried Sassoon and Wilfred Owen are actual characters in the novels. Anecdotes of horror and cruelty are scattered through the pages. Yet on the other hand her hero, David Prior, like Sassoon and Owen, decides that in the end he wants to return to France after being wounded, because that is the only place to be. They are the puzzle and despair of the full-throated pacifists. There is rather too much technical psychology in the books, centred round the character of Dr Rivers, and in *The Ghost Road* rather more homosexual sex than the plot demands. But she has added fresh insights to a theme which one might have thought by now was overflowing.

Thursday 8 May 1997, Fairmont Hotel, Dallas, Texas

Our only purpose in flying here was to interview George Bush, but it is soon clear that life has more in store. Dallas is proposing to entertain the Diplomatic Corps in this hotel and we are to be included in the festivities. Efficient and friendly ladies are bustling about with timetables and guest lists. George Bush is to be main speaker at lunch. Now we know why our interview was diverted from Houston to Dallas.

It is pouring with rain and I have two hours in hand. Once again, how unlike the life of a Foreign Secretary. I take a taxi to the Texas School Book Depository, not knowing what to expect. You buy a ticket near the entrance of this nineteenth-century warehouse and take a lift to the sixth floor. Suddenly, the drama is upon you. The radio announces that shots have been fired at the President of the United States. There are the cases of books, there is the sniper's window, there is the grassy knoll. Around you, brilliantly displayed, is the story of President Kennedy's last drive. There is no attempt to wrap up the mystery. Lee Harvey Oswald fired from this window and was quickly dead. Whether someone else fired and whether others were involved will never be fully known. During these visits to the United States I asked several people privately, not for the programme, whether they believed Kennedy would have carried forward his Presidency with the same élan into a second term. One of his Cabinet members answered that Kennedy would certainly not have allowed the United States to increase its commitment in Vietnam. But the general view was that there were flaws in the man and in his scene. The flame would have gone out anyway – though that is not to say that he would have turned out a bad President. Plenty of perfectly adequate Presidents had no flame.

I get back to the hotel in time for an alcohol-free reception in advance of an alcohol-free lunch. It still seems slightly strange for me to have lavish food without wine, but increasingly I get used to it and I suppose benefit from it. The bustling ladies are excellent at introducing me and then moving me on. I talk to the junior Senator from Texas, to the President of American Airways. Because of its geographical position and excellent airport, Dallas has become a national centre for many big companies. The Diplomatic Corps from Washington is a bit thin on the ground, but eloquently represented in the lunchtime speeches by the Ambassador from St Lucia.

George Bush gets an enthusiastic reception, which reminds me a little of the way in which Conservatives used to rise to Sir Alec Douglas Home after he left the Conservative leadership in 1965. A touch of guilt added to genuine affection produced standing ovations and tumultuous applause. George Bush, like Sir Alec, has the gift of conveying in plain informal language his mastery of international affairs. On NAFTA and on free trade in general he is notably liberal. When he commends his own son, the Governor of Texas, for a humane approach to illegal immigration, there is considerable applause, but the Republican Congressman next to me sits on his hands.

Upstairs the interview for the BBC turns into an informal chat. George Bush is a genuinely kind man and this influences his judgements on the past. He is sure that history will bring in a generous verdict on Gorbachev. We run through the history of the Gulf War and Bush's eventual success in bringing Congress and the Establishment into supporting his policy, which he claims public opinion itself always favoured. In the Gulf we achieved a 'coalition of the willing'. He worries that increasingly in the United States he sees a coalition of the unwilling, both on left and right. This coalition is a threat to the free-trade policies of the Administration, and also to the clear responsibility of the United States to pay its debts to the UN and support the new Secretary-General.

In the interview George Bush goes out of his way to pay tribute to John Major. He recalls how in the autumn of 1990 the British Prime Minister did not hesitate in giving full support to the United States, even though he had been only a week or so in office when the first decisions were put to him. He would have been justified in asking for time, but his support was immediate and continuous. Bush had made the same point vigorously in his lunchtime speech. The test of Anglo-American friendship does not come during cosy summits or well-orchestrated meals and speeches. It comes in difficult times when risks have to be shared or shirked.

We go through the story of the ending of the Gulf War. I recall that I was in the White House with him when Colin Powell came and reported that the pilots no longer relished striking the defenceless Iraqis as they poured, defeated, out of Kuwait. George Bush sets out with great force the reasons why he brought the war to an end rather than pressing on to beg Baghdad. His argument is convincing. If he and we had changed the purpose of the campaign we would have lost a large part of the coalition. We would certainly have lost the Russians, the British Labour Party, and many of the Arabs. George Bush thinks we would have lost the French as well. No doubt British and American troops could have reached Baghdad and overthrown Saddam Hussein, though with what casualties one cannot be sure. We might still be there today, sustaining the Iraqi regime which we would have put in place. We would have turned the Arab world into our enemies. This is one of the many instances where Professor Hindsight has his say, and gets it wrong.

Since George Bush has spoken so warmly about John Major

I ask whether he has telephoned him since our Election defeat a few days ago. He replies that he has sent him a letter but not yet spoken to him. 'Why don't we speak to him now?' he asks. Without waiting for a reply, he sets the call in motion. I have always found that high-placed Americans are hazy about the difference in time zones between the United States and Europe. Fortunately we get this about right and find John Major having supper at home in Huntingdonshire. For a few minutes the two men revel together in the pleasure of liberation.

Tuesday 20 May 1997, Washington

This is a day of memorials rather than live interviews. Memorials are the symbols of history, influencing those who will never again open a history book. The perception of a country's history by its citizens and by its rulers is crucial to the forming of its attitudes and policies. Considering the short history of Washington, the high proportion of memorial monuments to active buildings is striking. The Iwojima Memorial to the US Marines next to the Arlington Cemetery on the Virginian side of the Potomac is arguably the most dramatic of all. It depicts the Marines raising the Stars and Stripes over the captured Pacific Island, following a photograph taken at the time for *Life* magazine. Mark the cameraman and Bob the soundman argue quietly whether it is true that the *Life* photographer made the Marines re-enact the scene for the purposes of his photograph. Both agree that, even if this happened, it occurred immediately after the original hoisting of the flag and that several of the Marines depicted were killed in later fighting on the island. The heroic patriotism is entirely straightforward – quite different from the complicated mourning expressed in the Vietnam Memorial across the river.

One thing seems quite clear to me, the amateur. It is a sparkling Washington morning. The day before had been humid and murky. Now, behind the Marines, the slope falls to the river and the eye travels across to the George Washington Monument and up the great sweep of grass to the Capitol. We discuss whether the Capitol is two or three miles away. Just the ideal site and background for one of the PTCs (pieces to camera) for which Matthew and I have been preparing.

Quite wrong. Bob and Mark try different positions and different angles. I wait in the shade of some pines, watching blackbird fledglings snapping at each other, unable yet to fly. The preliminary verdict is that the light is hopeless. I would look like some dark Mafia villain. As they debate the scene becomes even more attractive. Two trucks unload a large contingent of Marine bandsmen in scarlet tunics and white trousers, together with their instruments. They form up just above the memorial. They have not brought any music with them. It becomes clear that they are there simply to be photographed, perhaps for a Memorial Day publication. Despite this added attraction the verdict is still negative – and absolute. We trundle downhill to the river. I hope that the New World Order extends to the blackbird fledglings.

Another monument, another attempt to deliver wisdom. There are two hazards at the Lincoln Memorial. The first are the planes rising from the Washington National Airport close at hand. These are, however, regularly timed and can be avoided with care. More difficult are the tourists. American tourists do not recognise me and are only mildly interested in TV cameras. British tourists recognise me; some say hello, others simply whisper knowingly among themselves. This is gratifying –

except that from past experience I know that one third of them are sure that I am John Major, one third that I am Geoffrey Howe and one third Douglas Hurd. The most intrusive groups come from the continent of Europe. They believe that they have seen me before and feel compelled to ask one of the team who I am. If this happens while I am in full soliloquy then we have to start from the beginning again.

These separate hazards mean that I have to climb the steep steps of the Lincoln Memorial several times, uttering my piece about America as the only surviving super-power. The punchline in this piece is: 'We are lucky in our super-power.' After about the fifth or sixth attempt I begin to feel that we would be even luckier in our super-power if it had not insisted on quite so many steps before one enters the cool, shadowy recess where the statue of Lincoln broods.

One of the advantages of using local camera- and soundmen is that they know exactly where to eat tastily at modest expense. The Mississippi catfish in the Georgetown Seafood Restaurant is memorable. After that a pause for me, while they go off secretly to film Robin Cook coming out of the West Wing of the White House on his first visit to Washington as Foreign Secretary. I do not think it is a secret from Robin Cook or indeed from the Americans. The secret is from other sections of the BBC, locked in a competition to film Robin Cook's first weeks in the Foreign Office. Strange are the workings of the internal market. It is thought that I should not be visible on this occasion. I use the time in the National Gallery, amazed all over again at the wealth of its European collections.

Woodrow Wilson's house in Georgetown is elegant, spacious and well cared for. But it is the house of a retired President, not an aspiring or ruling one. It was bought for him after he left the

White House, and is where he spent the last few years of his life, tended by his much younger wife, who stayed on here until her death in the 1960s. On one wall on the upstairs landing hangs a hideous design for the flag of the League of Nations. The cabinets are crowded with those ugly, rather expensive tributes which great men accumulate towards the end of their working lives. There are many photographs, including several of the British royal family, notably one of the President in conversation with King George V. That is *not* a conversation at which one would particularly have wished to be a fly on the wall. The tributes give only a pale impression of Woodrow Wilson's extraordinary sweep through Europe in 1919. The exhausted peoples saw in him the idealistic missionary bringing the casket of a just peace across the Atlantic which, when opened, would put an end to war for ever.

As I deliver my PTC I gaze at the President's portrait above the mantelpiece in the main upstairs room. The painting is well done, but gives nothing away. Intelligence, austerity and integrity are all present. What is lacking is the fire which launched the crusade and then spluttered out.

This was not planned in advance, but Woodrow Wilson is becoming perforce the central figure in these programmes. For British students of history the comparison is with Gladstone and the Midlothian Campaign, when the old man raised the nation against the Bulgarian atrocities being committed by the Turks. My sneaking sympathies have always been with Disraeli in that encounter. He tried to cope with the unprecedented spectacle of aroused public opinion, and at the same time to prevent the Russians from overrunning Turkey and cutting the link between Britain and India. But the difference between the two crusaders is as striking as are the similarities. Gladstone was in Opposition. It is not clear that his Midlothian Campaign saved the life of a single Bulgarian. Woodrow Wilson was in power; indeed, for a year or two he was the most powerful man in the world. His flight was higher and his fall greater. His concept of self-determination as the key to a just peace was flawed. So was his concept of the League of Nations. His country failed to support him, but even with American support he would have continued to stumble against the realities of Europe. There is another difference, however, which tilts the balance in Woodrow Wilson's favour. There was something in Gladstone's style which provoked accusations of hypocrisy. The portrait in front of me by contrast is that of a man of total integrity who climbed without reproach to the top of the tallest tree before falling disastrously to the ground.

Wednesday 21 May 1997, New York

Today we are filming at the Statue of Liberty. I am not quite sure why. Matthew says that it will be useful as a backdrop for anything the programme wants to say about the United States in general. It would also, of course, be equally useful for anything about human rights. It is strange how 'human rights' still sounds artificial in the English language. 'Liberty' or 'liberties' would be more historical and more resonant. I am sure the statue would agree.

It is not clear that we will actually get to the statue. When we reach our rendezvous on Battery Park at the bottom tip of Manhattan it is crowded with huge numbers of schoolchildren queuing for the boat. The service is suspended. It is easy to see why, for we are on the eve of the Memorial Day weekend. A procession of warships is making its way past the Statue of

Liberty through New York Harbour and up the Hudson River.

'One of yours,' says Mark, the American cameraman.

'Ah yes, a frigate; perhaps the guardship from the West Indies,' I say, not sure of my facts but glad to see the White Ensign.

Because of the queue it would take us several hours to reach the Statue of Liberty if we wait for the ordinary ferry. But Matthew is a quiet, persistent negotiator, powerfully backed by Bob, the soundman from Chicago. In the United States anyone with a TV camera tends to receive the exceptional consideration reserved in Europe for royalty. Within a very short time we are on board a cutter belonging to the Parks Service. Bob whispers that I must remember that for the purposes of this negotiation I am already a Lord and in sole charge of the London parks.

Liberty Island is whipped by a chilly breeze. This is not deterring the tourists now pouring ashore from packed ferries as the service resumes. Bob and Mark spend a happy twenty minutes organising the lighting. They warned me at the beginning that I would require huge reserves of patience in making this programme. This is part of the healthy slowing down of life which I have tried to practise since I left the Foreign Office. I look up at the statue and try to communicate with her. She is magnificent in a rather mysterious way. The famous inscription is concealed inside the plinth. I glance at a guidebook, and have an idea.

'Would you call those spikes or rays coming out of her crown?' I ask.

'Rays,' says Matthew firmly.

Soon we begin to record. This is not at all easy. The helicopters carrying the wealthier tourists around the harbour buzz with particular devotion round the statue. It is not possible to stop recording when a helicopter begins to obtrude, and then carry on again after it has moved on. We have to start afresh from the beginning each time the buzz occurs — or indeed each time an errant tourist wanders, munching something, between the camera and myself. Eventually I cut down the length of what I want to say, we frown at the tourists and set up a helicopter watch to find a relatively peaceful interlude. Then I begin.

'She has seven rays in her crown, standing for the human rights in each of the seven continents. But what do we do in the modern world if we find that human rights are abused? Do we——?' A group of tourists approaches and after I have stopped I realise that they are speaking Mandarin. It is still unusual to see freely wandering groups from the People's Republic of China. I am not sure that they are following closely what I say about human rights, but I take it as a good omen.

Friday 23 May 1997, The United Nations

The helicopter problem is even more dire in the garden of the United Nations by the East River. This would otherwise be an ideal spot for broadcasting. So our recording has to be done inside in the UN Building. It is more than forty years since I first got to know the Secretariat Building (vertical) and the General Assembly Building (horizontal). They have really worn remarkably well. As you go up the elevator from the entrance to the General Assembly, the tapestry on your left, presented by the Belgian Government, has faded graciously in the sunlight. Compared to the past there are many more bits and pieces of varying quality presented by member governments inside the building. There are also many more flags of member states to be raised at 8.00 a.m. each morning at the entrance.

New York is a city of remarkable glass palaces, and the UN is one of the earliest and most notable. Yet my memories of the building are on the whole gloomy. A large part of the four years which I spent at the UK Mission to the UN between 1956 and 1960 seemed to have been spent here listening to long speeches or waiting for bad news. The Suez Crisis at the beginning, the Congo Crisis towards the end, and in between endless debates on some of the world's trouble spots. Several of these, like Cyprus and Kashmir, are still troublesome. Others (South Africa, Algeria, West Iran) may still be troubled but no longer receive the annual attention of the General Assembly. My colleague John Thomson was the greatest living expert on the Cyprus problem. Here is the staircase under which he sat reading Thucydides in the original, waiting for the surge of Greek and Turkish oratory to spend itself. Here is the bench on which we sat during the Suez Crisis, taking it in turns through the night hours to record for a reporting telegram the vituperation of the world against Britain, France and Israel. Back after forty years I go up to the rostrum. The hall is empty except for three groups of whispering tourists right at the back. I make a speech from the rostrum solely for the BBC. It has never been easy at that rostrum to remember that you are speaking to the representatives of the whole world. The hall was never full for a visiting Foreign Secretary, and audience reaction is minimal. I used to take some trouble over this speech each autumn, revising and polishing the Foreign Office draft, simply because it was my annual pronouncement *urbi et orbi*. It came just a week or so before the much more challenging speech at the Conservative Party Conference. I need not have bothered. The most eloquent and telling phrases used to fall forlornly into that sparse gathering of pessimistic diplomats.

Time to keep our appointment with the new Secretary-General, Kofi Annan, on the thirty-eighth floor. He is brisk and practical, as neat in expression as in appearance. The room where we interview him suddenly becomes familiar. I recall one of the lunches which the Secretary-General traditionally gives each year to the Foreign Ministers of the permanent five members of the Security Council. Most of this lunch was spent arguing over the unnecessary communiqué which tradition required we should issue at the end. The communiqué contained nothing of substance, but that did not prevent an increasingly irritable argument about detailed phrasing. In the most polite possible way we began to irritate each other. Jim Baker became particularly impatient, with reason. Those who, like myself, believe passionately in diplomacy and the diplomatic method, have to acknowledge that it occasionally produces intolerable mealtimes.

As the camera is set up with the usual meticulousness I think of those of Kofi Annan's predecessors whom I have known. Boutros Boutros Ghali was a friend from early days when both he and I were Ministers of State for Foreign Affairs. Probably he should not have wanted to run for a second term. Both he and the Americans mishandled the tactics of his last few weeks, but his Secretary-Generalship was distinguished. He came in as a philosopher at a time when the UN needed a philosopher. Now it needs a careful but forceful administrator. I suspect it has got one.

The unfortunate Austrian Kurt Waldheim I hardly knew. We coincided once in the desert. The Sultan of Oman spends part of the year camped in the heart of his country, on his way from one capital, Muscat, to the other, Salalah. The Secretary-General of the UN called on the Sultan in the morning, the British Minister of State in the afternoon. As he was leaving and I was arriving we both felt the call of nature. We were given a Land Rover to drive the necessary few yards into the desert. The Secretary-General and I stood more or less side by side, peeing into the Empty Quarter. The Secretary-General was wearing a particularly European dark suit. No doubt each of us thought the other quite out of place.

My most vivid recollections of this thirty-eighth floor of the United Nations Building go right back to Dag Hammarskjöld during the years between 1956 and 1960. I used to come quite often to sit on the sofa in his office. This was not because Hammarskjöld felt a particular need to communicate to a junior Second Secretary in the United Kingdom Mission – I was accompanying my Ambassador, Sir Pierson Dixon. There were particular reasons why Dixon found it useful to bring his Private Secretary with him during his many conversations with the Secretary-General. Dixon, a scholar and outstanding diplomat, could himself be somewhat allusive and obscure. But the complexity of his thought and language was as nothing to that of the Secretary-General. Hammarskjöld's mind moved fast, but not in a straight line. His speech was full of historical and literary allusions which it was easy to miss or misunderstand. He had the habit of thrusting crucial documents under Dixon's nose for him to read briefly, while he himself continued the flow of exposition. His sentences were perfectly formed in English but pronounced with a strong Swedish accent.

These were not casual conversations. Many of them, particularly in the early years, dealt with Middle Eastern matters of huge importance to Britain. Dixon would have difficult instructions to carry out, but he would also be expected to convey an almost verbatim account of the conversation afterwards by telegram to London. He found it useful to take with him a Private Secretary who would sit silently on a sofa trying to memorise what Hammarskjöld had been saying. Nowadays, in an era of lower standards, Private Secretaries, sometimes more than one, sit scribbling shamelessly in notebooks during conversations of this kind. Forty years ago this would have been thought most unseemly. Hammarskjöld would certainly not have permitted it.

Hammarskjöld was himself a great scribbler of notes in pencil during meetings of the Security Council. I found a small batch of them in a drawer at home the other day. They convey the complexity and obscurity of his thought. This one was written in December 1956, just after the Suez Crisis passed its peak. R.A. Butler, in charge of the British Government, had evidently made some speech about the British role in the UN effort to clear the Suez Canal.

A statement like Butler's settles the issue in a way which makes it only a question of time (perhaps hours) when I must define the UN stand. This is possibly, in my view, a policy too much in line with the action from which it originally derives.

I hope that you are quite aware of what may be the end of this development for my part. I may feel that political casualties should be reserved for major issues.

The manuscript minutes which I exchanged about this with the Head of Chancery and with Sir Pierson Dixon show that we none of us were at all clear what Hammarskjöld meant.

Some of the same obscurity hangs over his reputation. He was a high priest rather than a ruler of men. Yet, even at times when the UN seems most talkative and empty, the reputation established by Hammarskjöld saves it from slipping into dust.

Monday 14 July 1997, Brussels

To Brussels by air to interview the Secretary-General of NATO, Javier Solana. He is in excellent form following the success of the Madrid Summit enlarging NATO. We talk alone for twenty minutes while the camera team make ready. He has become a friend. We worked closely together on Bosnia when he was Spanish Foreign Minister responsible for Spanish troops in that country. His views were always close to mine. We were together, without other allies, in the fraught negotiations at Ioannina on qualified majority voting in the EU before the Scandinavians and Austria were admitted. I am not surprised that he has done a good job at NATO. Solana is keen that NATO should be able to project security beyond its own frontiers, i.e. in the Balkans, though he believes that NATO will need more powers before it can do so effectively. This chimes well with what the Secretary-General of the UN said in May. We should not be frightened of accusations of neo-imperialism. If the UN and/or NATO are expected to clear up disasters inside individual countries they will need powers to run certain aspects of those countries as trustees until the disaster is over.

The NATO headquarters, halfway between the city of Brussels and the airport, remains deeply unimpressive. The Belgians offered it to NATO as a temporary makeshift when de

Gaulle expelled them from Paris in the 1960s; they have been there ever since. It was originally a military hospital and still has that air. Now that new members are to enter, and a shoal of non-members will be more closely associated, there is a case for a proper headquarters at last, though I expect the treasuries of the Alliance will unite against such an idea.

This new career of mine sometimes produces awkwardnesses. In the corridor I bump literally into the Italian Ambassador to NATO, who is an old acquaintance. He does not immediately know the correct protocol for addressing a former Foreign Minister who is pushing a trolley loaded with BBC camera and sound equipment. He took a liberal view; we talked for a few minutes about the internal affairs of Albania.

Tuesday 15 July 1997, The Somme

The skylarks are still there, and poppies scattered through the ripening fields of wheat and barley. The rolling countryside north of the Somme is more open, more hilly, more beautiful than I expected. Captain Douglas Hurd is buried in a small cemetery across the road from Bronfay Farmhouse. His gravestone is 2C, in the white dignified design of the Commonwealth War Graves Commission, different ranks side by side, linked by a straight line of red roses.

While the team is setting up I talk to the stout farmer in white shorts. He points across the farmyard to the barn which served as a hospital in 1916. Swallows swoop about its roof. It is clear from the documents that my uncle did not die painlessly from the sniper's bullet, as his Colonel wrote to my grandparents. He lingered on under that roof for two days. The brisk breeze, intermittent sunshine and occasional noise of a car on the road make the light and sound of television hard to control, so I have to repeat my piece to camera several times. On the road the signs mark Front Line 1 July 1916, Front Line 1 September, Front Line 1 November. The signs are only a mile or two apart. Over these sunny hills the British Empire slowly dragged itself forward, bleeding as it moved. I sign the visitors' book under the entrance arch and am glad that so many visit. Beautifully kept, Bronfay Farm is a place of deep emotion and dignity. I hope my children will come here.

We move north ten miles to the huge British Empire Memorial on the hill at Thiepval. We cannot film close to it because a British team with a big crane is cleaning the names on the inside walls. There are 70,000 names, men killed on the Somme but whose bodies were never recovered.

We move further to the ridge that the Ulstermen stormed on 1 July. A replica of the Helen Tower from County Down was erected here. I remember fierce paintings of the battle in Belfast City Hall. Then across a valley and railway line to the next ridge where the Canadian trenches have been converted into a park. But somehow the imagination cannot cope with this. It is not possible to recreate the horror. The trenches of 1916 are as green and peaceful as the pre-Roman fort above the Uffington White Horse where I walked last Sunday afternoon. Nature only needs a decade or two to distort history by smoothing it out.

We go back to Thiepval to film the memorial from below, out of sight and earshot of the crane. I talk about the change in ideas after 1916, from supposing that wars happen and must not be lost, to being convinced that war must never happen again. The first idea may have led to 1914. The second certainly led to the Second War in 1939. I think of adding a wrinkle to the thought. Those most determined not to drift into a second war seem to have been those like Neville Chamberlain, Baldwin and Ramsay MacDonald who never fought in the first. Those like Eden, Macmillan and Duff Cooper who actually knew the disaster of these hills and trenches turned away from appeasement before the end. I have not tested the thought and it seems too complicated for television.

Wednesday 16 July 1997, Geneva

A gentle UN bureaucracy sleeps by this lake; it is unlikely to be wakened by anything as soft as a kiss. The BBC arranged our interview by telephone, but passes and accreditation are needed. We have to collect these at 8.30 a.m. We halt in two successive car parks and pass through several uniformed officials, but arrive on time. The appointed office is empty. Ten minutes later a plump lady appears with a sticky bun and plastic mug of hot chocolate. Slowly she gives us forms to fill in and then yellow passes. She is not unhelpful, just slow. We leave her to consume the sticky bun, unimpeded by other duties.

Quite different is the interview with Mrs Ogata, UN High Commissioner for Refugees. She is the small energetic head of the only one of the UN fiefs at Geneva for which I have respect. The refugees whom she helps across the world are an index of its search for peace. While the cameras set up she tells me that her main concern is with Rwanda and the Congo. She is full of praise for her work with the last British Aid Minister Lynda Chalker and for Lynda's special knowledge of Africa. She believes that in 1994 and again in 1996 the UN and the West missed an opportunity to intervene decisively to stop the killing. Recently she made a strong philosophical speech at the Holocaust Memorial in Washington arguing that the great powers had a duty to intervene in the internal affairs of a country where there was mass killing. I press her on this. You cannot intervene one day and leave the next. You have to control and run most functions in a country if, in the face of disaster, your intervention is to achieve anything lasting. Mrs Ogata is prepared to be robust about this, and to accept the idea of temporary trusteeship. She is excellent news.

Back across the street to the Palais des Nations. Young UN officials chat happily on the grass, shaded from the heat by huge cedars. What do they actually do? The view of the lake and mountains is superb. There is an impression of permanent siesta. The main Council Chamber is decorated by fierce Spanish murals by an artist called Sert. It is not clear exactly what the massed slaves and soldiers are up to, but they make the comparable tapestry in the Security Council in New York look insipid. The Spaniards made this gift in 1936, by which time both Spain and the League were sinking to disaster. Political buildings tend to reach full splendour as their owners slide downhill – see the Viceroy's Palace in Delhi and the Parliament Building at Stormont. It is an argument against a new NATO building in Brussels.

Thursday 17 July 1997, Berlin

The Brandenburg Gate is losing its authority as it is built again into one side of a city square. It looks smaller and less imperial. In the same way united Berlin is losing the dramatic character of the two opposed halves. We film two pieces with the Brandenburg Gate as background – one on Bismarck; one explaining how there was no master plan for the world in 1989 after the Wall came down, just bits and pieces, like the Pariser

Platz now, full of tourist buses and books selling Red Army souvenirs made in Indonesia. I nip round the corner into the Wilhelmstrasse to see if Her Majesty's Government has yet started the new embassy building on our pre-war site. I chose the design from a display of models in the Foreign Office. No work yet. The Prince of Wales was not keen. I must watch this space.

We try to film at Checkpoint Charlie, which I saw hoisted into the air out of history in 1990, but it is now simply an American building site. We find a particularly grubby stretch of Wall daubed with lurid paintings. Then, on the spur of the moment, to Potsdam. I had wrongly supposed that the 1945 agreement between Stalin, Truman and Attlee had been reached in one of the main imperial palaces. No, Europe was partitioned in the Cecilienhof, a mock-timbered, much-creepered mansion dated 1916, now shared between hotel and museum. A quiet attractive park, beech trees and a lawn stretching down to the lake. It is hot and sultry, so I am allowed by my BBC mentors to film without a coat. Ray the cameraman lost a case of cables at Brussels airport. I am amazed by his calm under this, and the skill with which he borrowed replacements in Geneva, so that filming was not delayed. Work done, we eat frankfurters and ice cream under an umbrella in the adjoining *hofgarten*.

Friday 18 July 1997, London

Interview President Giscard d'Estaing in the sumptuous draw-ing room of the French Embassy in London. He decides to answer in French, which is right. Although his English is perfect and easy to understand, when speaking in French he deploys the full range of his voice and the mobility of his face and his hands. His analysis is coherent without being extraordinary. He is less attached to the presence of US troops in Europe than I am. His main concern for the future is the danger of 'convulsions' within states such as Algeria, about which the outside world can do little or nothing. Unusually for a Frenchman, he rejects the idea of a doctrine of intervention, even non-intervention, since circumstances will vary. No one seriously proposes to intervene in Afghanistan, whereas limited intervention in Cambodia worked and could work again.

In the afternoon we film for the second time in the Foreign Office. Robin Cook is away and I am allowed to use his office. Scruple prevents me from sitting at his desk. The room is becoming a little crowded. Malcolm Rifkind moved in a portrait of Palmerston, Robin Cook a bust of Ernest Bevin, rather larger than the one on the staircase. I read in the newspapers that the Nepalese prince over the mantelpiece, for many years the only picture in the room, is to be moved. There is no particular reason to keep him there, except that he is handsome and dressed in a yellow and green outfit which suits the colours of the room. I am glad that my private secretaries gave me a reproduction of him as a leaving present. The most tawdry object in the room is the globe, which I always meant to replace but there it still is, looking like something from Woolworth's.

Later we film on the staircase and round the bust of Anthony Eden. I suggested this five years ago and it was generously commissioned from Roy Noakes by Lady Avon and the House of Commons. The bust now has a much better backing than the one installed at the outset. I am anxious to describe Eden the brave, silvery saviour of peace whom we

Right *Harry S. Truman (1884–1972) became US President in April 1945 following Roosevelt's death. He educated himself and the American people in the essentials of world leadership.*
Camera Press Ltd

Left *Chiang Kai-shek (1887–1975), leader of the Nationalist Government in China. A world policeman on sick-leave.*
Popperfoto

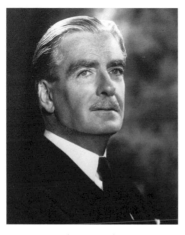

Anthony Eden (1897–1977) as Foreign Secretary: silvery, well dressed and almost always right. Then things went wrong for him and for Britain. Camera Press Ltd

Dag Hammarskjöld (1905–1961) was Secretary-General of the UN from 1953 until 1961, when he was killed in a plane crash in the Congo. Almost certainly a great man. Popperfoto

Below Gamal Nasser (1918–1970), President of Egypt, and a jubilant crowd after the withdrawal of British and French troops. Eden thought the Arab nationalist was a new Hitler. Camera Press Ltd

Chairman Mao (1893–1976) at the National Day Parade in Peking. On the right is Achmed Sukarno, President of Indonesia. Sukarno was a run-of-the-mill dictator. Amazingly, Mao smashed the institutions which he himself had created. Camera Press Ltd

Above *The birth of the European Economic Community. The Treaty of Rome was signed in March 1957 by Belgium, France, Germany, Italy, Luxembourg and the Netherlands.* Popperfoto

Below *President George Bush and King Hussein of Jordan. Condemnation of Saddam Hussein and support for the Allies was not universal. Western leaders worked hard to persuade doubtful Arab states.* Popperfoto

Right *Secretary of State James Baker. The craftsman of the coalition against Iraqi aggression.* Camera Press Ltd

Below *The author voting in the UN Security Council to adopt Resolution 678, which sanctioned the use of force against Iraq in defence of Kuwaiti independence.* Popperfoto

Mikhail Gorbachev (b. 1931) with John Major at 10 Downing Street. Gorbachev opened up his country and transformed its foreign policy, but could not move fast enough to save the Soviet Union, the Communist Party or himself. Camera Press Ltd

Above *Boutros Boutros Ghali with President Nelson Mandela. The events in South Africa after Mandela's release from prison in 1990 followed by the first free elections in 1994 have amazed and delighted the world.* Popperfoto

Below *The intervention of UN troops in Bosnia saved thousands of lives but could not stop the war. Here, UN soldiers escort refugees from the besieged Srebrenica in April 1993.* Popperfoto

Above *Conflict on the streets of Monrovia. The rival warlords have American names. Nothing else is reassuring. The Liberian Civil War was one of two dozen in progress in 1996.* Popperfoto

Below *One of the greatest challenges to present-day peace is international crime. Here, a Colombian soldier guards sacks of marijuana before they are burned.* Camera Press Ltd

respected hugely in 1954. Filming in the heart of the Foreign Office is difficult because of the echo of footsteps and the many angles from which people can unexpectedly step into the view of the camera. But there is nothing to match it, now that its full splendour is restored.

Saturday 19 July 1997, Belgrade

To Belgrade by British Airways, straight in white UN minibus to Vukovar. A Serb checkpoint, no-man's land, and into East Slavonia past UN and Croat flags. Croat flags with the distinctive chequer only raised this week as part of the gradual process of handing the area back to Croat rule. Flags not torn down as feared. For eighteen months East Slavonia has been administered by the UN, six months to go. The main town Vukovar is still 70 per cent destroyed. Summer sunshine and greenery soften the hideousness of destruction. The Serbs have held it since 1991, rebuilt nothing – shortage of money and of confidence that they would stay.

Straight to UN HQ. Shrewd to choose as the Administrator an American reserve general, Jacques Klein, born in Alsace, speaks French and German, understands that Europe is a mosaic not a melting pot. He talks fluently to camera about the job, which he enjoys. Pakistani and Jordanian battalions have just left, leaving him with Belgians and Russians, both high quality – though he had to read the riot act in Moscow at the start. Specialists from all nationalities. Gradually he is persuading the Serb majority here to take Croat nationality and vote in Croat elections. President Tudjman of Croatia has visited three times and played his hand well. Less progress with the two-way return programme. There used to be a small majority of Croats in a population of 190,000. The Serbs killed or expelled most of them in 1991. Serbs flowed in, expelled from their own homes in Bosnia or the west of Croatia – so now a big Serb majority in population of 130,000, many living in rubble.

UN policy is that everyone should go back to own homes – there are good records of who owns what. But why should a Croat who now has a job teaching in Split want to come back here to a ruined house in an area with a Serb majority? Why should a Serb living here among Serbs go back to the west – no job, surrounded by the Croats who kicked him out? But unless most do go home, this will remain a dissident Serb border region of Croatia, storehouse of future trouble.

Check into simple, clean hotel by the Danube, now swollen by rains in Central Europe. Drive to Klisa, the UN airbase, for jolly staff supper in hall built of containers, not quite proof against the thunderstorm which bursts as we arrive. Thai food. Sit at table with Klein, Armenian deputy, Portuguese adviser, Austrian police chief. That is the difference with other UN peace keeping – the UN actually *runs* this place, police and all. Functions gradually being transferred to Croatian Government or Serb local authority.

One day recently police chief came to Klein with long face. Terrible setback. What? Two of our police caught smuggling. Smuggling what? Cigarettes. Who? One Croat, one Serb. My dear colonel, you have achieved a breakthrough. If a Serb and a Croat can smuggle cigarettes together, we are halfway there.

No language can describe adequately the condition of that large portion of the Balkan Peninsula – Serbia, Bosnia, Herzegovina and other provinces – political intrigues, constant rivalries, a total absence of

all public sport . . . hatred of all races, animosities of rival religions and
absence of any controlling power – nothing short of an army of
50,000 of the best troops would produce anything like order in these
parts.

That is Disraeli, August 1878 – included by Klein in his briefing
– but evidently regarded as a challenge rather than an eternal
truth.

Sunday 20 July 1997

The Hapsburg Empire three centuries ago settled Ruthenes
round Vukovar to keep the Turks at bay. One more piece in the
European mosaic. Klein took us to Mass this morning in the
handsome (1907) Ruthene church in a village ten miles away.
Yellow lupins and blue scabious by the roadside, fields of
sunflowers nodding to the south. Ruthenes favour the Greek
Catholic rite, acknowledging the Pope but with married priests
and deep-voiced repetitious chant. This church has just been
re-opened after being desecrated by the Serbs, the village itself
unharmed. The choir in the bay just beside me turns out from
later talk to be farmers, led by one particularly strong voice
with seven hectares and grumbles about the shortage of
fertiliser.

Klein uses the priest's welcome to give a homily from the
altar steps, reminding the congregation that vengeance is the
Lord's and they should leave it to him. At the end we are joined
in the front row by two prosperous middle-aged men in slacks
and open shirts, whom I take to be village leaders coming to
talk to Klein. They turn out to be Bill Richardson and Peter
Galbraith, American Ambassadors to the UN and Croatia. After

Mass we all sit in the churchyard with repeated glasses of plum brandy while the school teacher tells us the history of the village and their present concerns. He thinks most of the Ruthenes who had fled will come back. He worries that the Croatian Government has drawn up a list of war criminals that includes completely innocent people. Then a churchyard picnic, served by ladies in embroidered dresses. I am generally held to be Lord Carrington, and made welcome.

On to a UN display for local children. Klein and I are drawn onto the football ground in a horsedrawn carriage behind a Pakistani pipe band. Klein is received with loud applause. Like the last Governor of Hong Kong, he eases his colonial task with notable political skills. Ukrainian and Serb teams parachute from the air, Russians pound each other with hammers, there is much ethnic dancing and huge quantities of hot dogs given free. It is said that the Serb team had planned to compete without parachutes because of their intense desire to reach the ground first. Finally we film round the Franciscan monastery and adjoining classical high school on the ridge above Vukovar. Evening swallows swoop among the handsome ruins. Must be the most destroyed town in Europe – except perhaps Grozny in Chechnya?

Monday 21 July 1997

A stork flies down the river bank. Attend 'morning' prayers at the UN headquarters. The head of each section reports developments over the weekend. A gypsy selling watermelons had complained that he was unreasonably prevented from entering the district. A house belonging to a Croatian lady recently returned from exile had been burned. Arson must be suspected in such circumstances, though the fire started in the roof, which usually means accident. The Serbs had complained that Croatian customs officers were wearing national insignia in a way illegal at this stage of the transition. They were right; the Croats must be told to stop. A Croatian minister was talking of the imminent return of 10,000 Croats to the district. He should be discouraged from raising expectations, since returns were occurring only a few dozen at a time, and there was no room for anything like 10,000 Croats until a comparable number of Serbs were allowed to return to their own homes in Croatia. Finally Jacques Klein had decided that yesterday's festival on the football ground was so successful that it must be repeated within a fortnight in the north of the district. But where would the hot dogs come from this time?

By Ukrainian helicopter to Sarajevo. A much bigger city, a bigger international effort, much more bustle and reconstruction. Cosmopolitan because of all the troops and aid workers. We spend the afternoon filming round the airport and at the meeting point where Bosnian Serb and Bosnian Muslim taxis meet to exchange passengers and goods. This is technically called the 'inter-entity' boundary, and is meant to fade away as the Dayton arrangements take hold and a united Bosnia emerges. Will it disappear or harden into something semi-permanent like the similar twenty-three-year-old line through Cyprus? Maybe in twenty-three years NATO or UN troops will still be patrolling this line through the seedy outskirts of Sarajevo as they still patrol in Nicosia.

The British Ambassador Charles Crawford arranges at a few hours' notice dinner with three leading Bosnian politicians, at the 'New Concepts' restaurant. After roasting me for five minutes about British policy during the war the Bosnians relax into optimistic geniality. They think there is a good chance of the Bosnian Serbs who favour co-operation gaining the upper hand over the extremists.

Tuesday 22 July 1997

Breakfast at Crawford's old-fashioned spacious flat with the British General Patrick Cordingly, who runs through the prospects. Ours is the second strongest contingent in SFOR, but not evident in Sarajevo itself. Troops will still be needed after the mandate runs out next summer, but we must not fall back into the position of 1993–1995, when we and others sustained the UN force and the Americans criticised from the other side of the Atlantic.

Quick tour of British Embassy. Staff expanded, building modernised, plenty of energy on all sides. Film in the old market, where mortar bombs fell. Now well organised and colourful in the sunshine. Buy roses, plums and bananas from a young man who has just been pushed back from Germany. Up onto the hill from which the snipers operated. Red-roofed Sarajevo spreads below, Florence with minarets, as it were. Finally walk across the bridge to the spot where the Archduke Franz Ferdinand was assassinated on 28 June 1914. So this chapter of history began. A small black and white post proclaims in four languages a wish for world peace – Amen.

CHAPTER SIX

TECHNIQUES

If, as I have argued, we will continue to live in a world of nation states that are both immortal and incompetent, then safety and progress lie in the ability of those states to work more effectively together than any of their predecessors. They will need to base all their actions on a studied grasp of reality. They will need to add to their grasp of reality a determination to preserve and build on the many hopeful elements in the world situation today.

Their ability to succeed will depend as always on a combination of power and ideas. Neither works in the long term without the other. If we try to disguise the importance of power because it can be unsightly, then we run into the risks of self-deception and illusion. That is why the last part of this book analyses the distribution of power in the world today and concentrates in particular on our remaining super-power, the United States of America. I shall try to assess to what extent power is likely to be used effectively to meet the different challenges to peace and security which we can now perceive.

But if calculations of power are essential so, one pace behind, is an understanding of the techniques of international diplomacy through which dealings between nations are organised. If the techniques are deficient then power and ideas, even great power in the hands of wise individuals, even ideas that are potentially persuasive, will falter and fail to take hold.

Effective policy making now depends to a greater extent than ever before on international institutions. Institutions are not simply meeting places for discussion, though they serve that purpose. They also increasingly possess powers of their own delegated to them by nation states. This is the pooling of sovereignty so angrily debated in Britain in the context of the EU, and in the United States in the context of the United Nations.

In his perceptive pamphlet 'The Post-Modern State and World Order' a British diplomat, Robert Cooper, accepts that the territorial state will survive because:

> The package of national identity, national territory, a national army, a national economy, national democratic institutions, has been immensely successful. Economy, law making and defence may be increasingly imbedded in international frameworks, and the borders of territory may be less important, but identity and democratic institutions remain primarily national. These are the reasons why traditional states will remain the fundamental unit of international relations for the foreseeable future, even though they may have ceased to behave in traditional ways.

Nevertheless Cooper puts his faith in what he calls the 'post-modern element' of the international system. He sees nation states as 'collapsing into greater order rather than into disorder'. He cites the Treaty of Rome and, more originally, the Treaty on Conventional Forces in Europe, as examples of nation states collapsing their sovereignty into international agreements policed by international institutions in order to achieve aims that lie beyond any one of them as single states.

My own experience has lain mainly within three of these organisations, NATO, the European Union and the United Nations. Even in the short span of my career I have seen each of these organisations acquire a characteristic flavour of its own. Because both the EU and NATO are in Brussels, it sometimes happens that a Foreign Minister will move within hours from a meeting of the Council of one organisation to the Council of another. There he will meet many of the same people and deal perhaps with similar problems. But because the institutions have evolved in different ways, they will be quite different kinds of meetings.

The NATO Council, for example, is a stately body with carefully prepared and formal speeches. The work of preparing decisions and of carrying them out rests with the sophisticated civilian and military under-pinning of the Organisation. There is no tension within NATO about the powers of the Secretary-General, the Military Committee or the Supreme Allied Commander. There may be lively debate about the actions that these authorities should take, but NATO is spared the institutional rivalries and anxieties that lie behind too many discussions within the European Union.

Nevertheless the European Union, at least in my experience of the Foreign Affairs Council, can provide a brisker and less formal exchange of views. The range of subject matter is much wider. Disagreements tend to be sharper. Decisions can be thrust upon you at short notice. I used to fly to Brussels on a Sunday afternoon in advance of an EU Council meeting on Monday, so that over a delegation supper on Sunday night I could go through carefully all the items on the agenda with our experts on the spot. The next day I would spend twelve hours, perhaps a good deal more, imprisoned in the Council building, as the Presidency tried to make progress on one item after another, reserving the trickiest for informal discussion over lunch. Over the meal ministers, deprived of their advisers, could be driven to concentrate on what they really wanted, forgetting the finer points in their written briefs. One had to eat, speak, listen and remember, all at the same time. These were testing occasions, sometimes enjoyable, sometimes thoroughly depressing. Even the most skilled interpreters cannot always bridge the difference between languages. The slower rhythms of NATO decision taking usually created less tension. In both organisations, barely glimpsed by the media or the public, the work of the Permanent Representatives who prepare the meetings and the trust between them is crucial. The public impression of ministers bravely launching their own ideas and arguments is carefully fostered by the ministers themselves, but rarely accurate.

A Summit Meeting of the European Union, formally called the European Council, is something else again. It occurs twice a year, sometimes more often under a feverish or ambitious presidency. Its ritual is now carefully established, beginning with general discussion, allowing the heads of state and government a private meal without their foreign or finance ministers, accelerating to decisions on the final morning. The presidency circulates to delegations at dawn on the last day its recommended conclusions, which will be published as soon as the meeting is over. Each President or Prime Minister confers hurriedly with his advisers as to the changes on which he should insist during the final meeting. The Prime Minister or President decides which arguments he will launch himself and which he will leave to his foreign minister. As Prime Minister, Mrs Thatcher always declared at the beginning of the morning that she was only going to concentrate on a small number of essential points. But she found it hard to follow her own advice.

Both Prime Ministers whom I served were adept, because of their own parliamentary experience, at this kind of fast-moving discussion. Other Prime Ministers and Presidents quickly wearied of detailed discussion of texts. Sometimes this led to their allowing points that otherwise they would have blocked. Sometimes it led them to penalise by negative decisions the British, who by prolonging discussion, were delaying their lunch or their plane home. Of all diplomatic occasions European Summits are the most exacting. They produce the same sort of nervous anxiety before and during the occasion as an important debate in the House of Commons. Few participants enjoy them.

The Security Council of the UN has its own atmosphere and rituals, closer to those of NATO than of the European Union. The General Assembly is quite another matter, particularly now that it is so huge and diffuse. Foreign ministers of the world gather in New York each autumn for the general debate. This is not a debate at all, since ministers do not take up each other's points. It provides an opportunity for them to give the Assembly and their own public at home a general survey of foreign policy. In the margins of the General Assembly at this time there takes place what can only be described as a diplomatic fair. Foreign ministers visit each other's booths and sample each other's wares. For day after day ministers hold bilateral talks with each other singly, or else meetings of groups such as the Commonwealth or the Permanent Members of the Security Council. Since Britain is the only country that belongs to all the major international institutions this coming and going becomes for us particularly intense. For example, the annual diplomatic fair in New York was the occasion where I traditionally met the Chinese Foreign Minister to go over at length the problems of Hong Kong, and the Iranian Foreign Minister to go over much more briskly our differences with that country, particularly the *fatwa* against Salman Rushdie.

Despite this multitude of international organisations it is sometimes necessary to create a new forum for particular purposes. For example, we were in 1990 faced with growing difficulties over German unification. The German Chancellor was understandably anxious to press ahead fast because he saw a window of opportunity that might close. The American, French, Russians and British had some status in the matter as occupying powers under the Potsdam Settlement. The last three of these four had some public doubts; their heads of government nursed strong private misgivings. There was no way in which all this could be sensibly thrashed out until the Americans ingeniously proposed the two plus four grouping of the two Germanys and the four occupying powers. It was a prime example of procedure helping substance. Thanks to the meetings in different capitals of this group over following months we were able to establish certain points which, if left unresolved, would have caused great difficulty – for example, that the united Germany would be fully part of NATO, and that the Poles should have a Treaty and not just an informal arrangement defining their western frontier. The doubts were answered and the misgivings smothered.

The second example occurred over Bosnia. Since the EU, the UN and NATO were all involved one might have thought that nothing more was needed except decent co-operation between these three. But it was not enough. We badly needed a small forum in which those immediately concerned, including the Russians as well as the Americans, could thrash out differences and try to chart progress. The Contact Group was invented for this purpose, and was essential for keeping the main players in some semblance of co-operation up to the Dayton Agreement of November 1995. The Contact Group continued to function during the Kosovo crisis of 1998 because once again it became essential to keep the Russians involved.

All these organisations function under the searchlight of the media. We have moved perforce into the world of open covenants openly arrived at, of which Woodrow Wilson dreamed in 1918. The difficulty is that the media in democratic countries are not so much interested in the covenants as in the battles. They tend to regard these meetings as jousts for armoured champions, rather than opportunities for agreement. This inevitably affects the behaviour of the champions. They learn to relish the moment when, in the cool of the evening, they can lay their armour aside and explain to their own national press how valiantly they thrust against the enemy. This exercise may be necessary for their survival, but if they are too self-indulgent in preening themselves at the expense of their foreign colleagues their influence over those colleagues will soon weaken. Nevertheless, since most agreements take the form of a compromise, a minister has to get up early in the morning and broadcast often if he is to convince that he has not surrendered essential interests to foreigners, who are by definition more wily and unscrupulous than himself. Ministers from all democratic countries have to wrestle with this problem in one form or another. In the European context it has been particularly heavy for British ministers, who tend to be regarded by their interlocutors as particularly cunning and well-briefed, but by their fellow countrymen as hopelessly outclassed and consistently outmanoeuvred.

In the modern world communication has become astonishingly easy. When I joined the Foreign Service in 1952 a typewriter would only make four or five copies of a document, and the last one was smudged. The tedious process of ciphering and deciphering telegrams meant that brevity was greatly prized. Any substantial Foreign Office document had an identity of its own. It was clothed in a jacket that showed how it had passed from one hand to another. Now it is possible to communicate messages of great length almost instantaneously. Ministers can pick up a phone and communicate directly with anyone across the world. Technology has abolished all except the last two obstacles to total communication. The first remaining obstacle is that there are only twenty-four hours in a day and seven days in a week, of which human beings require to spend a certain proportion asleep. The second is that the human brain is only capable of assimilating and retaining a certain quantity of ideas and information. These two limitations put great power in the hands of those who sift the information before it reaches the decision takers. In a world of instant global communication the

Private Secretary and the Chef de Cabinet have entered into their inheritance of power.

Ministers of the major powers now work in a constant snowstorm of information. They are required to take within hours, often more or less in public, decisions which their predecessors were able to mull over for weeks in private. When I began to write this book some commentators were looking away from this overburdened array of Western institutions to what then seemed a more subtle, less formal system which had begun to operate in Asia. We were invited to admire the way in which Asian countries, operating in much looser institutions such as ASEAN, relied on personal relationships rather than bureaucratic structures and did not bother much about transparency or democratic accountability. The Asian miracle seemed to embrace not only phenomenal economic growth, but also a more flexible form of political co-operation. That myth has been exploded by the Asian currency crisis. The Asian form of co-operation proved ineffective, and was worsened in some countries by the habit of ignoring democratic opinion, which some Westerners, particularly businessmen, had hailed as proof of Asian good sense. Those who argued that the people of Asia were not interested in democracy but only in a full rice bowl have found that lack of democracy has helped to empty the rice bowl. In his book *East and West* Chris Patten rams this point home inexorably. The West certainly needs to improve its methods of co-operation, but there is no longer an Asian model from which we might admiringly borrow.

The fact that information, like money, washes in huge quantities about the world every hour of the day does not reduce the need for human beings in authority to meet. Since Tolstoy wrote *War and Peace* people have argued about the extent to which individuals shape the affairs of the world. Individuals in authority, and their courtiers, tend to exaggerate their own significance. But the character of such an individual, and the chemistry with which he or she relates to others, can be of crucial significance if the call is close. As I have already said my rule of thumb used to be that personal trust and personal relationships added or subtracted about 10 per cent to or from the chances of success in an enterprise. Some individuals, for example Chancellor Kohl and President Yeltsin, are more closely affected than others by their own personal relationships. The influence that one practitioner can exert over another depends not just on his or her own ability, but on the information available on what is going on at the other side of the hill. Charm and intelligence are unlikely to succeed unless they are supported by insights into the hopes and anxieties of the negotiator across the table. It is the essential job of the professional diplomat to supply these insights.

In the world of immortal but incompetent nation states professional diplomacy becomes more not less important. Professional diplomats have always been easy targets for criticism, and need to find modern terms to justify their continued usefulness. It is not enough simply to talk in the jargon of their profession about the cultivation of 'friendly bilateral relations'. I used to cross this phrase out when it came up in drafts of minutes that I was invited to send to my colleagues, particularly those in the Treasury. It is a phrase replete with that cosy vagueness that makes outsiders suspicious of diplomats. They need to be more specific.

Their first task is the accumulation and use of relevant information. On the whole embassies are not now needed to report immediate and dramatic events. The news of a coup, a terrorist attack, even a substantial famine, will be flashed across the world without benefit of ambassadors. But the modern media are far less competent in the routine reporting of ordinary events, of what is actually said and done. Television is confined by the sound-bite. The written press, at least in Britain, has deteriorated in quality. Readers are confronted each day with acres of comment and gossip about abroad, but a dearth of actual reporting of what has occurred. If the British Foreign Secretary wishes to know what President Chirac or Chancellor Kohl actually said on a particular occasion, or the content of one of their decisions, it is no good looking to most British newspapers. He needs an agency tape backed up by a report from the British Embassy in Paris or Bonn.

The second main function of a diplomatic service is negotiation. This is the best known and has changed least over the years in fundamentals, though it now occurs more often within the agenda of international institutions. Particularly when it is successful diplomatic negotiation attracts little attention, but continues to be as technically demanding as ever. I recall as haphazard examples from my own experience the long-drawn and painful negotiations with the Chinese about the new Hong Kong Airport, the negotiations with Argentina about fish and then about oil around the Falkland Islands, and the negotiations that brought Denmark back on board, dripping but safe, after her people rejected the Treaty of Maastricht in their first referendum of June 1992. All three examples were traditional negotiations, involving technicians and lawyers brought together under the leadership of professional diplomats, and in the final stages requiring continued efforts of well-briefed politicians who had built up a relationship of trust with those with whom they were dealing.

In each of these three cases the result was satisfactory to British interests. If I had to single out a particular operation for technical complexity I would pick the third example mentioned above. The different layers of diplomatic action over the months in all European capitals, the ballet of legal argument, the sensitive relationship with Danish politicians and public opinion, the handling of parliamentary opinion here in Britain, the use of the British presidency to focus attention, and finally the triumphant performance of the Prime Minister John Major at the Summit in Edinburgh in December 1992, when he handled several tense subjects simultaneously from the chair, should be a model for study by budding diplomats. I shall not forget those three crowded winter days in the Caledonian Hotel and Holyroodhouse or the talent and energy of the team which we deployed.

Professional diplomacy is thus needed to provide not facts and figures but the relationship between those facts and figures, together with insights into the likely behaviour of those who take the resulting decisions. Repeatedly in the modern world the government of a nation state needs to protect a particular national interest, but also in its own interest needs an international agreement − whether on a security matter, on trade or finance, or increasingly on the environment. The professional diplomat can suggest and carry through the means of reconciling these national needs. Because these means will almost certainly involve compromise, the diplomat will rarely be a popular figure. It will often be suggested that he should have stuck it out and fought for one hundred per cent of the national interest, or that disagreement would have been preferable to the compromise that he reached. He will be vulnerable both to the idealist who believes that men would be brothers if diplomats would only let them alone, and to the blinkered nationalist who believes that his representatives should stay away from market places in which they will always be outwitted by dishonest foreigners.

But the diplomatic process will go on day by day, forum by forum, because it is necessary. The worry is not that diplomacy will decay but that it will be overburdened. There are already too many international institutions and far too many international meetings. It is easy to create and difficult to abolish such institutions and meetings. Heads of governments and ministers are beset by minor proposals that should either be settled at a working level or abandoned. There is much frantic discussion of detail, too little leisurely development of personal trust and analysis of fundamentals. These problems of overload and overflow, common to all the international institutions, have to be overcome. They are signs of immaturity in institutions that are still early models of their type. The emphasis on subsidiarity within the European Union, the effort to simplify the G8 summit meetings, the stable-cleaning of the Secretary-General of the UN show that the point has been grasped though not yet fully acted on. It would be worth dedicating one regular meeting of each international institution every two or three years to the examination of what it should stop doing. But the excess baggage that these institutions and their operators sometimes carry do not obscure the fact that their journeys are necessary.

CHAPTER SEVEN

THE FOURTH CHANCE

Previous page *Over the years, massive diplomatic effort has been put into the Middle East peace process. President Clinton watches as PLO leader Yasser Arafat and Israeli Prime Minister Yitzhak Rabin sign an accord to expand Palestinian control on the West Bank. Rabin was assassinated on 4 November 1995 by an Israeli extremist opposed to his efforts to secure a peace with the Palestinians.* Popperfoto

We now have our fourth chance. For the fourth time since the Congress of Vienna enough debris of the past has been carted away from the building site for us to see the outlines of a fresh opportunity. The fourth opportunity is different from the first three in as much as it does not follow a catastrophic war. This time it was not a country or an alliance that was overthrown, but a system of government. The collapse of Communism was not accompanied by devastated cities or armies of refugees. The world was not for the third time in ruins. There was not the same immediate compulsion to a radical restructuring of the world as drove the statesmen at Vienna, at Versailles, at Yalta and Potsdam. This fourth chance in the search for peace is thus even more complex than those preceding it. Some say that there was never an opening, others that we have already lost it. It is certainly true that we are proceeding at the pace of a tortoise. It is just conceivable that we shall make more lasting progress in this way than our predecessors who were compelled to stake all on the great leaps into the unknown that they devised after those three wars.

The threat to peace has changed – changed but not disappeared. There will always be those, after some sudden turn of events, who hope that the pressures of suffering have actually forced human nature into a new mould, squeezing out the greed, hatred and fear that in history have been the main incentives to violence and war. But looking across the international scene today I can see no evidence that this has occurred, no ground for hope that in this world the lion will lie down with the lamb.

The threats remain, but are of a different kind. Between 1814 and 1989 individual states, sometimes alone, sometimes in alliance with others, pursued their national objectives. Wars occurred when one or more of those nation states judged that their objectives could no longer be pursued by peaceful means. This type of threat certainly remains, though in modified form. Future wars between nations are less likely to result from a clash of giants pursuing national objectives than from adventurism, probably of a medium-sized dictator possessed of the instincts of a gambler. The attack by the Argentine military dictatorship on the Falkland Islands was followed eight years later by the attack of Saddam Hussein on Kuwait. The failure of both these adventures is a good sign for the future. It was not easy in the autumn of 1990 to put together the wide international coalition against the Iraqi aggression, and it was even harder to keep it together. Of course the blindness and bloody-mindedness of Saddam Hussein made it difficult, though not quite impossible, for anyone outside Iraq to argue for compromise. But the quality of President Bush's leadership carried an important and hopeful message for the future. That American leadership was not itself adventurist. President Bush, like Margaret Thatcher, concluded soon after the invasion that war would be needed to force Saddam Hussein out of Kuwait. But he instructed Jim Baker, his shrewd Secretary of State, to lead the rest of us in a search for a diplomatic solution through the UN which could have averted the bloodshed. Moreover, the President stayed constant in his objective, even at the end when the Iraqis had been beaten. If the Americans had then changed objective by adding the overthrow of Saddam Hussein to the liberation of Kuwait, then trust in American leadership would have dissolved in the Arab world and in Russia, and with it the coalition that won the war and has contained Saddam Hussein ever since. The steadiness and good sense of American leadership throughout the Gulf crisis made a deep impression on those of us who had to join in deciding what share of the risk we ourselves would shoulder.

Neither the Argentine military nor Saddam Hussein used nuclear or chemical weapons, though the latter had done so earlier against Iran. We have yet to face a threat from an adventurer who has acquired the knowledge and the matériel with which he could threaten his enemies with a nuclear attack. We shall be lucky if we get through the next few decades without some such threat. The reasoned anxiety about North Korea makes the point.

The threat to peace may not come from a state at all. The nineteenth century was familiar with terrorism but not on a scale or with the complexity with which we live today. We are better at analysing terrorism than defeating it. It may be fired by fanaticism as, for example, with certain types of Islamic fundamentalism. It may be induced by greed, for example by the appetites of the drug barons. Or it may simply be a device, as with the terrorists in Northern Ireland, to achieve by killing people what they have failed to achieve by persuading them.

But the most pervasive spoiler of peace in recent years has been neither the adventurist dictator nor the terrorist. The most virulent plague has been civil war – the more depressing because we are not in sight of a cure. Collective security can halt the adventurous dictator. Rigorous international co-operation can do something to check the terrorist. But outsiders cannot compel people to live at peace with each other within their own country. Nor can governments in this world of free markets effectively control the huge quantity of cheap weapons now available to anyone who wants to kill his neighbour or is fearful of being killed by him. There have been ninety civil wars since 1845. Two dozen were in progress in the middle of 1996. There is something particularly desolate about a country in the grip of civil war. The most pitiful capitals that I visited as Foreign Secretary were Beirut, Mogadishu and Sarajevo.

It is usual to say afterwards: 'You should have stopped it before it started'. It is easy to generalise about the need for preventive diplomacy. But each civil war is different in its origins and character. In Lebanon political and religious differences came together to explode the carefully constructed constitution that had kept Christians and Muslims together. After the Lebanese had destroyed much of their country in civil war their natural Lebanese commercial instinct began to reassert itself in favour of compromise and peace. But by this time Lebanon was caught up in the quarrels of Palestinians, Israelis and Syrians so that the Lebanese are no longer in charge of the future of their own country.

Africa is particularly subject to civil war because of the nature of African frontiers, often drawn in the last century by European statesmen anxious to compose their own differences, like noblemen negotiating the boundaries of their personal estates. It would not have occurred to Lord Salisbury or Bismarck or Delcassé that they were drawing the frontiers of future nations. Yet when the colonial empires were dissolved the Organisation of African Unity proceeded to insist on the old colonial boundaries. The new African leaders saw clearly enough that only rarely in Africa could diplomats find tidy frontiers containing peoples with enough shared identity and interest to hold together. It was better to make do with the haphazard frontiers drawn by the colonial powers than to start a task of revision that was bound to be unrewarding and dangerous.

The result, perhaps inevitably, has been a rash of African civil wars. Some, as in Nigeria, Namibia and Mozambique, have been in the end composed by a mixture of exhaustion and outside diplomacy. Angola has teetered for years on the edge of a settlement, Congo on the edge of disintegration. Liberia has virtually collapsed and so has Somalia. In both countries the struggle is not one of tribes or ideas, but of warlords who succeed only in destroying what they are attempting to conquer. They make a desert, but cannot even call it peace. Western aid cannot restore collapsed institutions and public services so long as there is fighting among the ruins. In 1997 and again in 1998 Albania showed that this was not purely an African illness.

Bosnia was something else again. Tito drew the boundaries of the different republics inside Yugoslavia in a way that left large numbers of Serbs living outside Serbia in Croatia and Bosnia, and large numbers of Albanians living inside Serbia in

Kosovo. It is facile to say with the benefit of hindsight that Yugoslavia, or indeed Czechoslovakia, were failed creations. They were attempts to solve particular ethnic problems in the centre of Europe and they succeeded for several decades in the middle of the century. When Czechs and Slovaks decided to live apart the separation was quick and peaceful because there was little or no ethnic intermingling. No such neat solution existed in Yugoslavia. A Yugoslavia divided on purely ethnic lines would have left only a small Muslim state in Bosnia and a patchwork of districts in Serbia. The international community came to roughly the same conclusion as the OAU in Africa – that it was better to recognise existing frontiers, however imperfect, rather than try to redesign them. The Bosnian Serbs, egged on by Belgrade, refused to accept that they should live in peace as a minority alongside Bosnian Croats and Bosnian Muslims inside a state called Bosnia. I have never thought this was inevitable. It is unfashionable to say so, but Yugoslavia may have been within a decade or two of reaching break-even point, that is the point where too many people had too much to lose in terms of prosperity for civil war to be feasible. But Yugoslavia by enforced authority failed before Yugoslavia by consent could become a reality. As one Yugoslav friend put it to me, the peoples concerned carried too heavy a burden of history for their ship to reach harbour. Slovenia escaped with a ten-day war. Kosovo is in turmoil as I write; Macedonia has so far survived uneasily. The war between Serbia and Croatia, being essentially a war between countries, was brutal but not sustained. The war in Bosnia, being essentially a civil war, lasted for three savage years until brought at least temporarily to an end by exhaustion, effective sanctions against Serbia, and increased Western military intervention. The Bosnian War was not the most destructive in the world in terms of lives lost or blighted, but being fought between Europeans its horrors and crimes aroused particular shock and frustration as they were relayed night by night into every Western living room.

These, then, are the main dangers that the international community now has to face. 'International community' is a handy phrase – does it mean anything? A large part, probably the greater part, of international diplomacy now takes place within the framework of one or other of the international institutions made familiar by the initials of its cumbersome full name. Do these institutions add value to the nation states of which they are composed – or are they simply a series of stages on which the member states play out their ancient games? As often happens in life, the cynical answer is no longer the realistic one. The UN, NATO, the EU, the WTO are all painfully and slowly building a character and an influence that go beyond the elements of which they are composed. They are still far short of turning into reality the rhetoric that surrounded their birth and fills their founding documents, but one by one they are gaining useful weight.

This weight is gained by the wish of their members. They remain fundamentally organisations of member states. Their battalions, their dollars, the influence of their resolutions depend on decisions concerted in New York, Geneva or Brussels, but originally taken in the capitals of member states and in particular of the great powers.

The concept of nations coming together to negotiate agreements has been familiar since nations existed. What is new in this century is the decision of nation states to establish international institutions to carry out those agreements. These institutions are not monsters hungry to eat up the nations, as some Americans imagine of the UN and some Britons of the EU. They are designed by nations to carry out agreed purposes that individual nations know they cannot accomplish alone.

That is why the question 'Who are the great powers?' remains relevant to any assessment of the modern search for peace. In 1997 the United States is certainly the only super-power. Only the United States has that mixture of wealth, military strength and determination that can make a country potent across the world. But three other candidates for super-power status present themselves for the next century – Russia, China and Europe.

Russia occupies a huge land mass. She has a large and skilled population and an amazing array of natural resources. Nevertheless the thought that in the twenty-first century she might be a super-power rests mainly on the fact that she has been one in the past. From the second half of the eighteenth century until 1917 Russia was indisputably one of the great powers of Europe, made more formidable because she was through this period building an empire in Asia. After the Bolshevik Revolution and a civil war she disappeared briefly from the world stage, but at the same time was working out a missionary doctrine of formidable strength.

This missionary element is new in the equipment of a great power. Even the most excited of British or French imperial thinkers did not suppose that the whole world would one day be red (or green) on the map. True, the Jacobins carried the French Revolution beyond national borders, which was why they were detested and in the end defeated. True, the British sang 'Wider still and wider shall her bounds be set', but this was not a doctrine that would ever have appealed in practice to Lord Salisbury or even Disraeli, let alone Gladstone. There remains a strong missionary flavour to American foreign policy, but it cannot compare with the absolute certainty of revolution that underlay Soviet doctrine. When Khruschev said 'we will bury you' he was not announcing an aggressive policy, simply stating the conviction that Communism was bound to prevail revolution by revolution, and as a consequence establish the Soviet Union as the leading world power. Stalin knew how to use this doctrine without himself being dominated by it. He fused the convictions of Communism with the ancient patriotism of Russia. For a few years it worked. I remember vividly listening to the daughter of one of the generals whom Stalin murdered in 1937. The young girl knew that her father had been innocent and that Stalin had killed him. Yet when Stalin died in 1953 she and her sisters cried bitterly because he had won the war and made Russia great. The patriotic girls wept for the Communist murderer.

For Communists, the death of Stalin was as powerful an event as the death of John Kennedy for the Western world. The ruthless apparatus of power created by Stalin and bequeathed by him to his successors horrified and frightened the world for forty years. Yet it was becoming hollow within. Fewer and fewer of its practitioners believed what they were taught and what they taught to others. When it came the collapse was quick and total.

It is sometimes more difficult to rebuild from ruins than from clear ground. I once opened a school in west Kenya that was simply a stone shed – without furniture, without books. All it had was a crowd of enthusiastic pupils. At about the same time I went to Alma Ata, capital of the new state of Kazakhstan. At first sight they had a big advantage there over Kenya – plenty of investment, infrastructure, equipment, teachers. It was just that they were all wrong – wrongly designed, wrongly installed, wrongly trained. I felt sometimes that the reformers there would rather have inherited nothing, a blank sheet, than the corrupted Soviet legacy.

The rebuilding of Russia from among these obstinate ruins will take a long time yet. Neither economic nor political progress will be steady in a straight line. Russia needs leadership but also democracy, and the combination is unfamiliar to them. They will find their own way, and the influence of the rest of the world on that process will be marginal.

During this long period of reconstruction the Russians will continue to regard themselves as a great power. The imperial as well as the Soviet legacy give them this status in their own eyes, and we would be wise not to deny it, not least but not only because Russia remains a nuclear power. The missionary element has gone. Russians no longer expect to teach the world a universal lesson of their devising. They no longer expect to dominate, but they insist on being consulted. If the Russian Government is taken into the confidence of the West, then we can within reason rely on its understanding and support. We found this in the Gulf War and in Bosnia. The Russians no longer expect to hold a veto over what we do, but they believe they have a right not to be surprised. 'No vetoes no surprises' was the phrase that I worked out with my Russian colleague, Andrei Kozyrev, to summarise this relationship.

In the old days the Soviet Union exerted its influence across the globe. Now that the missionary spirit and the economic strength have disappeared, Russia is no longer intimately interested in what happens in Congo or Angola or Somalia. It is tactful to allow her a role in the Middle East peace process, though she no longer commands the allegiance of client states. But around her own borders she remains anxious and suspicious. The countries of the former Soviet Union used to be called 'the near abroad' in Moscow. The phrase is no longer politically correct and has fallen out of use, but it accurately describes how many Russians feel about their former subjects and new neighbours. As the world-wide missionary vocation of Communism drained away, the older Russian concept of spheres of influence resurfaces. This is partly because millions of Russians live outside the present borders of Russia. The way Russians are treated in say Ukraine or Estonia will remain of lively political importance to the occupant of the Kremlin. But for many decades yet there will be a deeper feeling that the countries immediately to the south and west of Russia fall within a special sphere of Russian influence. I do not believe that Soviet tanks will ever roll into the streets of Tallinn or Kiev as they once did in Budapest and Prague. But if we have any historical sense we will understand that this feeling, however incorrect, is inevitable and we will handle our own policies accordingly. That is why the timing and method of NATO enlargement is so important. Russians do not seriously believe that NATO is fashioning a dagger to be thrust into the heart of Russia after the manner of Napoleon or Hitler. But they believe that they do have a special interest in the future of at least the countries that were once part of the Soviet Union. This is an interest that we would do well to accommodate for the next decades. This will be the main Russian concern outside its own borders and the limit in practice of its claims during the next twenty or thirty years to the status of a great power.

The doctrine of spheres of influence has an old-fashioned ring. It is part of the old order condemned after the Great War by Woodrow Wilson. But we need not be afraid of the idea provided it is not an excuse for barbarism or bullying. Military and economic reality ensure that whatever the rhetoric Russia will in fact for the foreseeable future exercise greater influence than anyone else over most of the former members of the Soviet Union. We need not deny this. We have to manage the military dimension of our relationship with Russia so that she can no longer persuade herself that she can profit from foreign military adventures. At the same time, we have to weave a complex relationship with the newly democratic Russia, bringing her slowly into most of our institutions. If we handle this process right, the pull of the West on Russia will remain much more powerful than the pull of China, because our rope will have more and thicker strands.

China also lives with a mixture of Communist and imperial legacy. Indeed the imperial ingredient of China's legacy is older and more deeply rooted than anything devised by the Czars. Peter the Great and his successors borrowed without shame from the West, whereas the Chinese emperors, right to the end of the dynasty in 1911, pretended that in all important matters China was self-sufficient. To some of the Czars at least the outside world was inhabited by foreigners whose skill and experience could be usefully borrowed. To the Chinese emperors it was inhabited by barbarians who should be kept at bay and confined, first of all to Canton and then perforce to other ports designated by treaty. It was only for the purpose of paying tribute to the Son of Heaven that emissaries like Lord Macartney could be admitted to the presence of the Emperor. There is no equivalent in Moscow to the Altar of Heaven in Peking, which is the centre of the world. Nor does the Kremlin radiate absolute and secret power in the same way as the Forbidden City, whether directed by the Emperor or by Chairman Mao.

When the Chinese Empire collapsed through its own

hollowness the Chinese experimented between 1911 and 1949 with different blends of nationalism and capitalism. Chiang Kai Shek, like Peter the Great, was not ashamed to borrow from the West and acknowledge the debt. But the result in China of this process was quite different – corruption, warlords, humiliation by the Japanese, a long and destructive civil war. The nature of Chairman Mao and of his Communist victory, combined with the underlying imperial legacy, gave the People's Republic of China from the outset a self-confidence that it has never entirely lost. We know now of course of the inner struggles within the Forbidden City during those early years of Communism. We know the immense cost to China of the Great Leap Forward and then of the Cultural Revolution. I can think of no great ruler other than Mao who remained a revolutionary even after the revolution had brought him to the top of the heap. Napoleon had himself crowned Emperor by the Pope and surrounded himself with the traditional apparatus of a European ruler, including a Hapsburg princess as his wife. Mao by contrast broke the mould which he himself had created and smashed the institutions of his own People's Republic.

Through the years no other country has left so emphatic an impression on me as China. I lived there for two years as a young diplomat in the mid-1950s and have been there often since. No one who ever saw them will forget the huge parades of a million people in front of Mao Tse-tung as he stood on the Gate of Heavenly Peace, military on 1 October, civilian on May Day. We walked in the Western Hills round Peking in the mid-1950s, before the peasants had been drilled into uniform responses. They were quite ready to criticise the Communists to us in those early years for their interference and their high taxation. But at least, the peasants said, we now harvest what we sow, whereas before the liberation bandits came down from the hills and took our crops under the pretext of one political slogan or another. Out of those impressions I have never believed and do not believe now that the People's Republic is likely to disintegrate. When pushed to the point its people will decline to exchange the present order, however tyrannical, for a return to warlords and anarchy.

Under Chairman Mao and his successors the foreign policy of the People's Republic has been ruthless but defensive. The diplomacy has from time to time been grandiose. China sought to put herself at the head of the Non-Aligned Movement. Chairman Mao spoke as if China alone, because of her huge population, could survive a nuclear war. But China has not tried to impose Chinese rule or stir up a Communist revolution across Asia since the defeat by the British of the Communist insurgency in Malaya in the early 1950s. Neither has China used the existence of large influential Chinese minorities in Asia as a tool for subversion. The wars in which she has engaged, in Korea, against India, against Vietnam, have been ruthless but limited, designed to fortify the security of China itself.

Of course it is possible that this policy might change as China at last turns her huge potential into economic and military strengths. Conceivably as that strength develops she might throw off the cautious diplomacy which has been so marked, for example in the Security Council. She might attempt to impose her own solutions on the problems and divisions of Asia.

Certainly she is most unlikely to let Tibet go or renounce her ambition of bringing Taiwan under mainland rule. She may become an increasingly awkward neighbour. I doubt myself if that awkwardness will expand into a serious challenge to the way the world is run. China has a huge way to go before she can rival the strength of the United States. Indeed the more prosperous China becomes the more she has to lose from both war and indeed the fear of war which would deter investment and trade. Mao's triple slogan: 'Dig tunnels deep, store grain everywhere, always resist hegemony' is not an adequate prospectus for a neo-capitalist society. Whether Marxists were right or wrong about the imperialist scramble for markets in the nineteenth century, in the twentieth and even more in the twenty-first centuries, capitalism, including Chinese capitalism, is a force for peace.

The main problem facing China has nothing to do with foreign affairs. If her move towards capitalism is irreversible then she will need to find some way of modifying the Communist political system. I do not believe that she can indefinitely run a liberalised economic system where people are encouraged to travel, make money, take risks, and at the same time deny those people any say in choosing their government or any right to express their opinions. The problem for Hong Kong is that the flags changed before the Chinese on the mainland had resolved this paradox. The story of China in the next decades is unlikely to be smooth or straightforward, but it is also unlikely to amount to an assertion of global power.

We shall need to draw China, like Russia, towards accepting the rest of the world's norms for conducting international relations. This will only work if the Chinese accept these norms as advancing their own interests. In the long run they will not gain by cheating on copyright or selling dangerous technologies to dangerous dictators. But as part of this unwritten bargain we have to accept that the Chinese will find their own way of running China. It is not for us to design blueprints for the future of the People's Republic. This does not prevent us from persistently nudging the Chinese on questions of human rights as we nudged Brezhnev's Soviet Union, or from showing them that a policy of Chinese military expansion would carry severe penalties.

What about Europe as a great power? The founding fathers of the European Community were good strong Atlanticists. Jean Monnet spent some of his most successful working years in Washington. But he and his disciples certainly envisaged Europe coming steadily together into a United States of Europe, which would as an entity be roughly equal in wealth, in power and global reach to the United States of America.

The Gaullist variation of the original vision provided for less integration, but also for a more open rivalry with the United States. That coincided with the mixed distrust and envy of America which provided one strand of European political thinking in the 1950s and 1960s. Fear of American nuclear policy then coincided with anxiety about what seemed to be ruthless incompetence in Vietnam. Although that anti-American strain has greatly weakened in the 1980s and 1990s we still find Europeans who talk as if Europe can be ranged over and against the United States. We saw it for example at the beginning of the Bosnian crisis when the Luxembourg Foreign Minister, another staunch Atlanticist, allowed himself to give the impression, as President of the European Council of Ministers, that Europe could look after the crisis by itself. We hear the same note again in some of the unpromising efforts to promote the Euro as a world reserve currency that might oust the dollar from its present pre-eminence.

But experience has shown that the relationship between Europe and the United States has to be a lot more subtle than that. We need to draw the right rather than the fashionable conclusions from what happened in Bosnia. It is not true that the European Union was paralysed by internal divisions. On the contrary, we agreed on a limited form of intervention combined with strenuous humanitarian and diplomatic ingenuity. I recall no European foreign minister arguing forthrightly for the alternatives, for a policy of doing nothing, or for a policy of intervention to impose a solution, or for a policy of lifting the arms embargo and letting the parties reinforce themselves and fight it out. The tragic difficulties lay in the former Yugoslavia, not in Brussels. Nor would it be true to conclude that Europe was useless and the United States, single-handed, saved the day. In Bosnia, as has happened before and will happen again, the outcome depended on the United States and Europe working together. Neither could manage without the other.

The tormented relationship between Israel and the Arabs gives another example. The European Community acted as one in 1980 with the Venice Declaration, at a time when there was no peace process and something of a diplomatic vacuum. The Venice Declaration's reference to Palestinian self-determination irritated the Americans but it gave substantial help to those Arabs who believed that a reasonable outcome for the Palestinians did not have to depend on yet another war. When George Bush and James Baker took a firm initiative the Europeans were content to sit back and support. They grumbled from time to time over points of protocol and American habits of over-statement. But so long as the Americans remain seriously engaged in a peace process, without tilting too far towards Israel, the Europeans should be ready in support with their diplomacy and their finance. We should have too much sense to suppose that any European interest would be seriously served by putting forward a separate and complicating initiative in the Middle East simply in order to display a European label. If the American effort dribbled away or became hopelessly one-sided Europe might have to take a hand of its own.

There is everything to be said for Europeans acting together whenever they can reach agreement. That agreement should be attainable over a steadily increasing range of subjects. As usual the danger is excessive rhetoric. There is no reason why the European Union should have a common policy on the Falkland Islands or the Central African Republic. The fact that we cannot agree on everything should not discourage us from agreeing on as much as we can. There is no reason why agreement should not be possible on the main questions of world security. For example, there is no difference of principle or interest that need prevent the members of the European Union from working out and putting into effect together a common policy towards Russia. But this policy cannot in practice be implemented in isolation from the Americans. The nature of the Atlantic relationship is such that a successful policy requires Europeans to work alongside the Americans rather than in distinction from them. This is quite compatible with questioning American policy or even occasionally challenging it. Such questions and challenges may be treated as evidence of hostility unless the underlying relationship is deeply rooted in partnership. A partner is not the same as a subordinate, and the more closely the Europeans can work together the more partnership and less subordination there will be in their dealings with the Americans. But Europeans should, and almost certainly will, accept that so long as American foreign policy retains its present general character, American leadership within an Atlantic partnership is desirable in the search for world peace.

So whether we like it or not the United States will remain for the foreseeable future the only valid super-power. It follows that the nature of United States foreign policy is crucial for all of us. Whichever way we look at the problems of the world, the question stays fundamental. What do the Americans mean by leadership? In US foreign policy more than that of any other country, the tension between idealism and realism is continuous and striking. The most emphatic spokesmen of the United States deny that there is any such tension. Here, for example, is President Carter:

> *I was familiar with the widely accepted arguments that we had to choose between idealism and realism, or between morality and the exertion of power; but I rejected these claims. To me, the demonstration of American idealism was a practical and realistic approach to foreign affairs, and moral principles were the best foundation for the exertion of American power and influence.*

But of course this will not quite do. In real life a great power, let alone the only super-power in the world, is faced, perhaps at intervals of months rather than years, with a series of practical choices, the answer to which depends on the relative weight given to national comfort and national security on the one hand and the claims of idealism on the other. Sometimes it is the realists who pose the question. What does the great power do when its own security requires a forward policy which might be seen as unjust or aggressive by others? Many see that as the test set in Vietnam. Certainly in its dealings with Latin America over the years, the United States has from time to time plumped for a forward policy in the old-fashioned national interest at the expense of idealism. More often nowadays the question is put by the idealists. What does the great power do when there is evil loose in the world and suffering on a disastrous scale, but when the effort to end the suffering and achieve peace with justice is costly, dangerous and perhaps unsuccessful? It is by that question from idealists that the United States is likely to be tested in the decades ahead.

Of course this predicament is not confined to the United States. The same tension ran through British foreign policy, particularly in the nineteenth century. It was, for example, at the heart of the debates between Gladstone and Disraeli. In the 1870s the realistic British national interest was seen to include the protection of the Ottoman Empire against the Russians. The collapse of the Ottomans would enable the Russians to separate Britain from her Indian Empire. The idealists saw the atrocities that the Turks were inflicting on their subjects in the Balkans and elsewhere – Armenia, for example – and clamoured that something must be done. It was the British rather than the Americans who bequeathed to the India of Jawaharlal Nehru the habit of clothing foreign policy in moralistic generalisation.

We have recently seen in Britain a small re-run of an ancient debate following the claims of the Labour Government elected in May 1997 to pursue a uniquely ethical foreign policy. I say a *small* re-run because the main characteristic of Labour foreign policy has been continuity, not change. On all the principal issues which vex the world the new Government have carried forward the policies which they inherited. They have made the mistake of trying to pretend that the relatively minor changes which they have made add up to a new and morally superior approach to international affairs. Reality has already exposed the hollowness of this claim. The task of an intelligent and tough-minded Foreign Secretary, Robin Cook, has been made more difficult by the scale of his initial pretensions. This is a function of the adversarial nature of British politics, rather than evidence of some new British third way through the maze of conflicting considerations with which the world's statesmen wrestle.

Modern German foreign policy has achieved some of the same character by a different historical route. I remember Hans-Dietrich Genscher taking me aside during some argument over the Balkans and asking me to remember that because of its past Germany could never afford to be found on the wrong side morally of any particular diplomatic question. In Bosnia the British and the French, two peoples in whom idealism had been tempered over the years by worldly realism, found it from time to time irritating that they appeared to be taking the risks on the ground, while Americans and Germans expressed their anguish and disapproval from a detached distance.

So the Americans are not alone in having to reconcile idealism and realism. It is certainly inaccurate to describe the idealistic strain in American foreign policy as hypocritical. On the contrary, it is deep-rooted and widely shared by the American people, which is why American leaders, both Republican and Democrat, constantly resort to the missionary rhetoric of America as uniquely equipped to lead the world against injustice.

This tendency is sharpened by the growth and intensity of modern communications. There has been a remarkable spread of instantaneous knowledge without any corresponding spread of responsibility. Television brings suffering into every living room. Democratic politicians come under immediate pressure to cope with man-made disasters of whose origins they may have been totally ignorant even a few days earlier. Pity and indignation play a much larger part in international life than ever before. Their constituents and the pressure groups that sway their constituents ask consistently for justice as well as for peace. But is justice only to be sought when the injustice comes within range of television cameras? In any case what is justice in Jerusalem or Kabul or the Brcko Corridor or indeed Belfast? Do you, for example, arrest alleged war criminals in the name of justice if by doing so you provoke a fresh outbreak of fighting, more killing, more crimes? Often those who ask these questions sound cynical or evasive when matched against the white-hot flame of indignation. But the moment a government or an alliance moves from just indignation to policy making, these are the sort of questions that assert themselves.

Truman was the first United States President to accept openly his country's new role. In 1952 he left office with these words:

> *We are at the top and the leader of the free world – something that we did not anticipate – it is a responsibility which we should have assumed in 1920. We did not assume it then. We have to assume it now – it is our duty under God to continue that leadership in the manner that will prevent a third world war.*

In that task the United States has succeeded. The danger of a third world war has receded almost to vanishing point. But the United States finds that it cannot lay down the burden. The new tasks are less weighty but more complicated. Less weighty because the President of the United States is not having to worry day by day whether his leadership might involve the world in a nuclear war. More complicated because the United States is not now confronting an evil empire but a host of smaller, more intricate problems, many without either intellectual or moral clarity.

There is a strand in American thinking that makes it particularly difficult for the United States to handle these problems. True, she wields overwhelming economic and military power. True, her leaders and her people have an instinct against tyranny and injustice. But they have another instinct which leads them to distrust entanglement. America succeeded precisely because it separated itself from the old world, from the complications of the balance of power, from the discredited system of secret diplomacy, risky alliances and dubious compromises. America was better than the rest of the world, partly because it had distanced itself from that world.

This sense of separateness is no longer expressed in open isolationism, but it has not disappeared. If you tune in to the news bulletins of middle America or study its newspapers, if you listen to its congressmen and consider their background, you find that foreign affairs are a long, long way away. Powerful lobbies insert themselves into this silence on behalf of particular ethnic groups, but the noise which they make is no substitute for broader democratic discussion. There is no sustained interest among large numbers of people in the intricacies of the problems that the State Department and the President have to face. When a dramatic disaster pushes a particular country into the headlines that prominence is likely to be brief and the reaction to it simple. It is much easier simply to support the unity of Ireland and remember the great famine of the 1840s than to analyse what the people of Northern Ireland actually want. It is much easier to support Israel than to worry about how Israelis and Palestinians are to live together in a dry and narrow land. It is much easier to pick a good guy in Russia or in the Balkans than to carry through day to day a policy that does not depend on ephemeral personalities. This lack of a sustained public or congressional interest in foreign affairs makes life hard for the policy makers, a difficulty intensified by a constitutional system that separates the elected Congress from the men who run the White House, the Pentagon and the State Department.

Perhaps the clearest illustration of this is also the most important, the handling of the relationship with China which we have already mentioned. Chinese policy makers think long. Their own internal arguments take place in private. They control absolutely their own media and they are not bothered by their domestic public opinion. Faced with this opponent across the table the United States cannot afford to fluster, to drop cards on the table, to doze off, or alternatively to shout words of angry abuse. The United States needs a cool, calculated policy towards China, preferably bi-partisan, that it can sustain through all kinds of temporary commotions and excitements. The United States cannot ignore the lack of human rights in China, for to do so would be to deny part of its own character. The United States certainly cannot ignore its commitments to Taiwan or to the independence of other Asian countries. But it cannot allow either human rights or Taiwan to dominate exclusively its policy towards China or its discussions with Chinese leaders. Getting the balance right is what the policy has to be about, even though some Americans believe that there is something immoral about deliberately striking a balance between ideals and reality. For its part the US can reasonably expect the Europeans to stop regarding China mainly as a market and begin taking her seriously as a power.

CHAPTER EIGHT

WHERE FROM HERE?

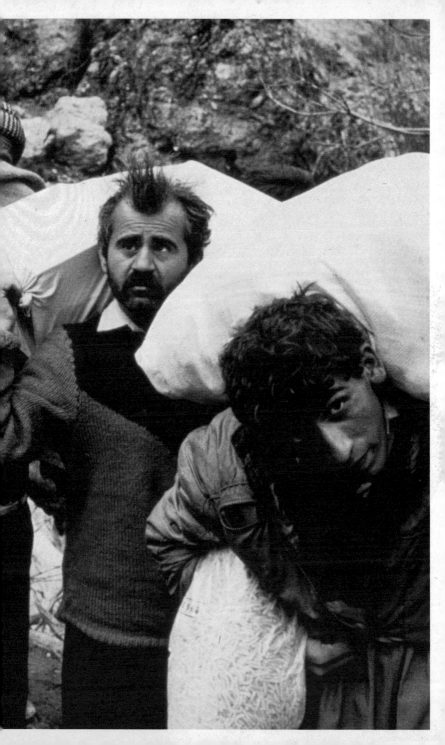

Previous page *Over a million Kurds fled from Saddam Hussein's brutal repression of their failed rebellion in 1991. Here, Kurdish refugees cross the Uludere mountains from northern Iraq into Turkey and Iran.*
Popperfoto

I have tried, in the previous chapter, to analyse the main dangers to peace in coming decades, the relative weight of world powers and the instincts in policy making of the surviving super-power. If my analysis is right then the most frequent test of policy making will come through the outbreak of civil wars across the world with their attendant savagery. On each occasion a wide spectrum of choice is in theory open to the United States and the rest of the international community. At one end of the spectrum is the imperial or MacArthur solution. In 1945 General MacArthur took over the collapsed society of Japan and remade it in a different image. He acted briefly on the principle of the Roman Imperium or the British Raj. When Cabot Lodge, as Ambassador in Vietnam, organised the fall of Ngo Dinh Diem's

Government he was playing a semi-imperial role, just as the British did in Egypt when they surrounded the King's Palace with tanks in 1942. It seems to me highly unlikely that the United States will ever plump again for a choice at this imperial end of the spectrum. There will never be a Pax Americana enforced across the world by legions despatched from the Pentagon. Even in tiny Haiti the American choice was much more temporary and limited. Nowadays it will be the idealists rather than the soldiers who will favour the use of imperial force (always denying that adjective) to root out injustice, topple criminals from power or revive collapsed societies at considerable risk and expense. They will not often prevail.

At the other end of the spectrum is the choice of doing nothing. From time to time that is the way the decision will go. No one in the United States has bothered much about the civil war in Tadzhikistan. The Americans put only a tiny effort into Afghanistan, which savage war has crippled for eighteen years. When I visited Georgia I found a country in which few houses were not marked by bullets. One civil war was still in progress, another was dormant, and even in the rest of the country there had until recently been plenty of internal violence. Yet the concern and activities of the international community was slight – except for the action of Russia asserting in practice, if not in theory, the doctrine of a sphere of influence. It costs a lot to put a television crew into such distant countries, so public opinion is hardly roused. The issues are complex, the risks clear and the exit route from any intervention is doubtful. It is no good expecting from the United States or from any of us a clear-cut, consistent set of rules.

Statesmen may try to apply a universal standard on all occasions, but they will never entirely succeed. A tragedy needs to be obvious before in a democratic country an expensive or risky effort can be made to deal with it. The test of statesmanship in these situations is to spot a danger before it becomes tragic when remedial steps can still be small and safe. The difficulty is that such steps require in international law and in practice the consent of those in power on the ground. Those on the ground rarely welcome impartial foreign intervention until they despair of dealing with the problem themselves. Such despair usually comes later in the day.

This brings us right up against the paradox with which we started, namely the reality of a world of immortal but incompetent states. In the early days of the United Nations member states were passionately jealous of their own sovereignty. For many of them this sovereignty had only recently been acquired as the colonial empires dissolved after the war. Article 2(7) of the UN Charter provided against any intervention by the UN in the internal affairs of a member state. 'Nothing contained in the present Charter shall authorise the UN to intervene in matters which are essentially within the jurisdiction of any state.' The rule was neglected so far as South Africa was concerned, because it was felt that apartheid was uniquely abhorrent. The Article was held not to apply to the remaining colonial territories such as Algeria or Portuguese colonies in Africa which were frequently debated. But overwhelmingly intervention by the United Nations was held to be justified only when the government of the state concerned had requested it. Indeed, the immediate cause of the Six Day War between Israel and her Arab neighbours in 1967 was the decision of the UN Secretary-General U Thant to withdraw the UN emergency force which separated Israeli and Egyptian troops simply because President Nasser of Egypt had withdrawn his consent for their presence on Egyptian soil. The fact that the abandonment of the international effort led to war was not held in 1967 to override the supremacy of a nation state in deciding what foreign troops should be stationed on its soil.

Since then the situation has changed dramatically. The principle of intervention on humanitarian grounds is now widely acknowledged and put into effect. Yet the results are imperfect and horrors persist, mainly as a result of conflicts inside a country rather than direct acts of aggression committed by one country against another. So the pressures for yet further intervention multiply. I could quote many examples, but will choose a press article based on a lecture given by Mrs Ogata, the UN High Commissioner for Refugees on 30 April 1997 in Washington. It is worth underlining that Mrs Ogata is no extremist or unrealistic. She has shown herself to be realistic in handling the formidable range of her responsibilities across the world. Nevertheless she was moved to use these words, after paying tribute to progress that had been made in life-saving relief operations by the UN.

Why did it take until August 1995 before the people of Sarajevo and other besieged cities in Bosnia were saved by NATO and peace was pushed through? Is neutrality morally and practically viable in the face of widespread atrocities? Why was no country prepared to step into Rwanda at the height of the genocide in 1994? Why was the multinational force that had been authorised to come to the rescue of hundreds of thousands of refugees in eastern Zaire cancelled in December of last year? Thousands of people have perished in eastern

Zaire since then. The answer to these questions seems clear. It is because the major powers perceived no strategic interests or because their interests did not converge. In that sense the situation does not fundamentally differ from the Cold War years when political interests, stemming from ideological confrontation, were a cause for not halting the killing fields of Cambodia.

In my view there can be no true globalisation, if it is only economic, if we do not even reach out to halt genocidal situations. While respecting cultural diversity, true globalisation means universal respect for human rights, of the positive side of man, of the responsibility to provide protection against evil. That lies at the heart of refugee protection. Now, we have to take it one step further and be prepared to halt the worst evil at its source. That is my hope at the threshold of the next millennium. We need determined political leadership. We need citizens who are prepared to look beyond the domestic horizon and who can spur reluctant politicians into action.

I would disagree with Mrs Ogata when she says that the test which reluctant powers apply is whether their strategic interests are involved. If that were the test then Britain would not have sent troops to Bosnia or to northern Iraq or logistic battalions to Rwanda or Angola. In none of these areas did we have strategic interests. It is the view of all British governments nowadays that Britain has an interest in making a reasonable and realistic contribution towards a more decent world. Mrs Ogata is right, however, in saying that there have been differences of analysis between the powers about the nature of some of these problems. Such differences are inevitable.

The intervention by the UN in the Congo which began in 1959 was not regarded as a precedent to be followed. It was successful in holding the country together after the Belgians scampered out, but not in keeping it on an even keel. The results were controversial, and the cost immense, including the life of the Secretary-General Dag Hammarskjöld. Despite this experience over recent years there has been a marked shift towards intervention for humanitarian purposes by the UN in the domestic affairs of a member state. As often happens, practice has come before theory. The military intervention by Western troops in 1991 to help the Kurds in northern Iraq was a striking example. It was followed by the despatch of troops to Bosnia to protect international aid convoys. Both interventions were sanctioned by the Security Council. Characteristically the French were the first to feel the need to shape a theory to fit the practice. President Mitterrand commented on the expedition to northern Iraq: 'For the first time, non-interference has stopped at the point where it was becoming a failure to assist a people in danger.' His hyperactive Aid Minister, Bernard Kouchner, went further and talked of the 'devoir d'ingérence'. There was in his view not simply a right, but a *duty* to intervene.

As we have seen the High Commissioner for Refugees, with many others, has carried the thought forward and applied it in particular to examples of genocide. Genocide was widely defined long ago in the UN Convention of 1948. Under international law genocide covers a range of acts by one group against another falling far short of the mass destruction perpetrated by the Nazis against the Jews or by the Hutus against the Tutsis in Rwanda in 1984. If intervention to stop genocide is a duty, and if genocide is defined as widely as in the 1948 Convention, then there are at least half a dozen places in the world today where the UN should be taking or authorising military action against its perpetrators.

There is a mixture here of thinking from the nineteenth and twentieth centuries. Woodrow Wilson would have applauded the humanitarian zeal underlying this approach. But his concept of the League of Nations did not include armed intervention in support of its purposes. Public opinion properly mobilised should, he thought, be sufficient. In the nineteenth century the duty of intervention to stop pirates and slave traders was accepted. They had no difficulty in acknowledging that this involved gunboats, marines – and casualties. As Edward Mortimer points out in his shrewd pamphlet 'A Few Words on Intervention' (1995) John Stuart Mill considered earnestly in 1859 how far Britain should extend this principle, for example to help the cause of Italian freedom. As a conscientious liberal he became somewhat bogged down when it came to particular cases, judging that it would have been right for Britain to help the Hungarians in their resistance to the Russian intervention on behalf of the Hapsburgs in 1849, but wrong to help their original uprising against the Hapsburgs a year earlier.

Where are we now on this question of interference in the internal affairs of states? Few will now argue that it is never justified. We are all interventionists now. But that does not absolve us from answering certain difficult questions. They are the questions of the artisan rather than the visionary. But if they remain unanswered then we shall be in danger of raising expectations which we then do not fulfil. Our humanitarian instincts may sour into hypocrisy and failure unless we think straight from the beginning of each enterprise.

Who should authorise such intervention? That used to be the easy question. It should clearly be the Security Council of the United Nations. The composition of the Security Council and the existence of the veto can be criticised. But reformed or unreformed it was indispensable as a legitimising body. This was partly a matter of international law and partly of political prudence. A nation state would add substantially to the risks of an enterprise if it intervened militarily beyond its borders without the consent of the Security Council, even if it had obtained the request of the government that it was helping. But that rule of thumb only works if the permanent members of the Security Council usually abstain from using their veto to obstruct international enterprises on which most of the Council members are intent. It remains to be seen if that will stay true of Russia after the upheaval of August 1998.

Who shall carry out the intervention? A distinction is usually drawn here between peace making and peace keeping. Peace keeping is needed where there is a peace to keep. Warring parties reach some sort of fragile accommodation so that they are no longer killing each other, but there is no trust between them. They need an impartial outside force on the ground to police the cease-fire and prevent the killing from starting again. This has become a classic task for the blue helmets of the UN. These small UN peace-keeping forces, authorised by the Security Council, directed by the Secretary-General are now part of the world's furniture. The figures fluctuate. There were 80,000 of them in September 1994: at the time of writing there are 25,000. They do a worthwhile job, but they do not themselves solve the problem which is the occasion for their presence. They need to be accompanied by sustained and skilful diplomacy. Where this happens, as in Namibia, Mozambique and Cambodia, the UN scores a notable success. These successes tend to be forgotten while the failures remain to reproach us. The largest and most passionate flow of letters with the Foreign Office during my time as Foreign Secretary came in the first few months, as a result of the killings by Pol Pot and the Khmer Rouge in Cambodia, a faraway country of which we certainly knew little. The combination of a small UN force with international diplomacy backed by the powers most closely concerned produced an answer. Cambodia remains a troubled country with inadequate leadership and an anxious future, but it is no longer a flaming scandal.

There has been long discussion since the end of the Cold War about improving the ability of the UN to put a peace-keeping force quickly and effectively in the field. In our interview with him Brian Urquhart repeated the argument for a permanent UN force specifically trained for peace keeping. His background as midwife of many peace-keeping exercises gives him unmatched authority to comment. Brian Urquhart argues that it is now actually harder to persuade member states to contribute to a peace-keeping force than it was when he helped to put together the force that ended the Suez Crisis in 1956 or that intervened in the Congo in 1959. He finds it absurd that every time there is a fire the UN has to form a fire brigade from scratch. But no one is leaping to found a permanent fire brigade. The difficulty of expense speaks for itself. There is also the danger of Murphy's Law, namely that a force trained to keep the peace in tropical Africa might find its first test in Siberia. Under the leadership of Boutros Boutros Ghali the UN made some progress in pre-planning. It is certainly entitled to know in advance which nations are able and in principle willing to provide which skills and military resources at short notice. In the map room now installed at

UN headquarters there should at least be a list of telephone numbers across the world, behind each of which can be found authoritative national commanders whose instinct will be to help. The arguments against a permanent UN force do not apply against preparing logistical plans, standard operating procedures and competent military advice.

The most shameful episode of the Bosnian War resulted from the inability of the Secretary-General to raise sufficient extra blue helmets to serve alongside the British, French and others already in Bosnia in order to make safe in reality the areas that the Security Council had pronounced safe in principle. This failure, combined with the reluctance of the Bosnian Government to demilitarise these areas, made the concept of 'safe areas' unworkable. It should have been frankly rescinded on the grounds that the two conditions for its success had not been realised.

I recall visiting three UN peace-keeping forces – in Lebanon, Cyprus and Bosnia. The first two were both long established, and so far as I could see well run. But the corresponding diplomatic effort had run into the ground. So there they were, both stuck in unlikely places, unable either to achieve much or to pull out. It was in a bizarre way impressive to find a well-disciplined Fijian battalion camped on the barren hillsides of south Lebanon – and to watch Argentine officers shaking hands with the Queen outside Nicosia. The soldiers on the ground were always sure that they should remain, though year followed year (or in the case of Cyprus decade followed decade) without visible progress.

In the treasuries and ministries of finance of national governments it was argued that the presence of the international force actually hindered the search for peace by removing the pressure of fear on the local politicians to compromise. I hosted lunch for the leaders of the Republic of Cyprus and of the Turkish Cypriots at the Ledra Palace Hotel, placed exactly on the dividing line which runs through Nicosia. President Clerides and Mr Denktash were old acquaintances, almost friends. They had sparred with each other long ago as lawyers in the British colonial courts. They sparred with each other again over my lunch table, half in earnest, half in jest, both wishing to appear reasonable to the British Foreign Secretary without retreating a jot from their long-fortified diplomatic positions. I did wonder whether they would have continued this genial empty sparring if they had been told that the UN force would be withdrawing from Cyprus that evening. The news might have concentrated their skills on finding a way in which their two communities would live in peace together without blue helmets to keep them apart. But when I actually travelled the Green Line, escorted by the blue helmets through the narrow damaged frontier streets of Nicosia, between the defiant flags of each community, the other side of the equation prevailed. Take away the UN and the immediate result was likely to be, not a compromise between two elderly local leaders, but a violent smash and grab across the line followed perhaps by savage ethnic cleansing.

The British contingent to UNPROFOR in Bosnia was something else again. The Bosnian Serbs were not far away in the hills with their artillery but at that time in Vitez they were not causing trouble. The problem was tension between Bosnian Muslims and Bosnian Croats. In the town itself and the suburbs the two communities were hopelessly intertwined. Self-determination offered no clue, unless preceded by ethnic cleansing of a kind that the world rightly found repulsive. As in so much of Central and Eastern Europe the mosaic was the mosaic was the mosaic. New brutal memories and myths were piling up to strengthen fears and hatreds inherited from the past. The British troops managed day by day to defuse, to damp down, to keep the peace. Like a Roman legion they had built a long road up from their supply point in Croatia. They spent much of their time patrolling their road, securing it for the aid convoys to bring in supplies through the snow from all over Europe. Electricity had been cut off. The children played outside their houses and lit roadside bonfires in the dusk.

The British soon restored the power. But unlike a Roman legion the British blue helmets had no authority to annex a province or impose their own law or that of the UN. They operated in theory by the consent of the different Bosnian factions, in practice by small uneasy temporary pacts and compromises. They saved many lives. In the end the necessary consent in Bosnia fell below the minimum required for the force to continue. The Bosnian Serbs humiliated the UN and defied their own patron in Belgrade. They committed hideous crimes against those who were in theory their fellow citizens. The international community had stumbled into the foolishness of a ground effort directed by one international organisation and an air effort directed by another, with different rules, different membership and a different spirit. Eventually NATO disentangled itself from the UN, and the Bosnian Serbs provided a pretext for decisive air action. The exhausted combatants were hustled at Dayton into a peace agreement on lines that had been available to them for at least two years.

Several lessons emerge. Form a coalition (as in the Gulf) of like-minded supporters and keep it together. Keep your effort coherent under one command. Do not proclaim in public what you hope to accomplish until you are confident that you can carry it through. Be prepared to say no, to stay out unless and until you have that confidence and share it with all the main actors.

But the main question remains unanswered. Until it is answered, the hopes of the interventionists are to some extent hollow. This is particularly true of those who would most ardently press ahead, such as M. Kouchner and Mrs Ogata. How in practice can you reach your objective of peace with justice? It is not enough to say 'stop genocide' or 'respect human rights'. You will not achieve that objective by sending in troops for a week, or even by overthrowing a tyrant. After that you have to stay, and you may have to rule. This is the point that so often gets lost. The Bosnian disaster could only have been averted if in 1992 the Western powers with Russian acquiescence and UN approval had taken over the country by force and imposed peace. This would have meant Britain, France and the US incurring casualties. It would have meant telling the Bosnian Serbs and Bosnian Croats from a position of authority that they had to stay as part of Bosnia rather than exercise self-determination to join Serbia and Croatia. It would have meant ensuring that the Government in Sarajevo gave all communities a reasonable deal. Of course it is conceivable that different diplomatic tactics by outside powers at different stages might have produced a reasonable result without such a clear assertion of power – but I doubt it.

It is worth dwelling for a moment on the underlying philosophy here. Historians and politicians will argue for a long time yet on the merits and motives of those who created the Western empires in the last century. Certainly the better of them believed that they were acting in the best interests of the indigenous peoples, for example in deposing tyrants and stopping the slave trade; in creating sound administration, railways, famine relief and generally conducting a civilising mission. The colonial empires collapsed because leaders arose among the subject peoples who opposed that view and because the imperial powers ran out of the political and material energy needed to impose it against opposition. This experience is so recent and so controversial that, fairly or unfairly, it acts as a deterrent rather than a model for the kind of constructive occupation to which the logic of events now points. The new occupation could have none of the ambiguous motivation of the old. It would need to be limited in time and purpose, clearly aimed at building again local assets and energies which would make its own presence superfluous.

The only way to be sure of peace with justice is to go and enforce a version of that concept. Yet nobody proposed this. And no one would propose it in similar circumstances today. Many people, most of them far from the scene and not part of the limited effort which was made, willed the end but had no intention of willing the means – namely a war of intervention followed by a period of what might be called constructive occupation. This dilemma is certain to recur. What I have sketched is a semi-imperial policy. For many it carries unwelcome echoes of how the Roman Empire and later Western colonial empires were created. That is why most members of the UN would shrink away from it – quite apart from daunting questions of expense and casualties. American opinion in particular is far from accepting a doctrine framed in these un-Wilsonian terms. If that is true, then we may need to reinvent the concept of international trusteeship. Trusteeship is there in the UN Charter, but the cumbersome machinery there prescribed was applied only in the ex-colonies of the defeated powers. These procedures would need to be re-designed so that the UN can take into its charge (or entrust to the charge of a regional group) countries that have collapsed or are wrecked by civil war – as, for example, the EU has sought to administer the Bosnian town of Mostar. The American General Klein under UN command has had administrative responsibilities in East Slavonia. As we saw when we visited Klein he has handled these responsibilities with striking political flair. Serbs and Croats are learning to live together *because* for the past year or two neither of them has been running the place. These could be the first shoots of a new doctrine.

It is perfectly defensible in such cases, after examining the difficulties, to say that the international community can do nothing effective and must stay out of the way until those concerned have come to their senses. What is not defensible is to urge governments or the UN to intervene and then shirk the responsibility which may flow from intervention.

The same question arises whether the enterprise is run directly by the UN or, as in the Gulf and now in East Slavonia and Bosnia, in the hands of a group of nation states operating with the blessing of the UN. Even if the arrangements for putting together UN fire brigades were much improved, it is still likely that most peace-keeping enterprises above a certain size will be conducted either by an existing regional organisation, such as NATO or the Organisation of African Unity, or by a 'coalition of the willing', brought together *ad hoc* for a particular purpose such as the liberation of Kuwait.

So far we have been thinking of the threats to peace with

which we have been most familiar – aggression of one country against another and civil wars. But conflict between nations or even within nations may as the years pass be supplemented or superseded by other dangers. The globalisation of trade, finance and communications is bringing huge benefits to the peoples of the world. It would be perverse to deny this. Opportunities for increased prosperity and the opening up of individual lives multiply at an amazing rate. But the shining coin has another side. The same techniques enable criminals to organise their strength until it can exceed that of any state in which they operate.

They may be criminals devoted to drug running, to financial racketeers, to political terrorists or religious fanatics, or a combination of several of these. Powerful criminal organisations can permeate the institutions of the state, or defy them. They appear to be stronger than the Government of Colombia. They paralyse much of Algeria and loom large in several states of the Former Soviet Union. They will certainly absorb an increasing share of the energy and resources of international organisations. An international criminal court is on the way. It will not be of huge significance unless accompanied by co-operation in international policing and intelligence-gathering on a scale well beyond anything so far achieved. Those who pursue criminals must not be impeded by frontiers which the criminals themselves leap over with ease. The arguments for greater pooling of sovereignty and for authoritative international institutions may be much strength-ened as a result of this new set of dangers.

A danger unknown to our parents is the proliferation of weapons of mass destruction – nuclear, chemical, biological. In our generation we think mainly of nuclear weapons. That risk certainly remains, indeed it has been increased by the circumstances in which the Cold War came to an end. Nuclear knowledge and materials are no longer under the self-interested but firm grip of two disciplined alliances. But biological weapons may become the greater threat, being cheaper, more devastating, less detectable. The most intrusive powers assumed by the UN within a member state have been those entrusted by the Security Council to Ambassador Ekeus in Iraq. Saddam Hussein clearly had the will to use weapons of mass destruction against his enemies; the international community decided that he must be denied the capacity. The detailed supervision of existing weaponry and possible future capacity is backed not just by the continuation of existing sanctions but also by the threat of renewed military force. It is the toughest peacetime stance that the UN has ever taken. It is made realistic, incidentally, by a pooling of national intelligence data at the service of the UN which is also unprecedented in peacetime and significant for the future. This robust international intrusiveness has been relatively easy to achieve because Saddam Hussein's past record is in everyone's memory and he makes no pretence of penitence. A less punitive robustness is being used to deter the eccentric North Korean regime from nuclear proliferation. It remains to be seen whether these two examples will set the tone for international responses in the next century – or whether, as in the past with Libya, the United States may feel driven to cut corners, use its own power and expect afterwards to be met with general relief rather than indignation.

These are dangers and remedies spanning the world. In his book *The Clash of Civilisations*, Professor Samuel Huntington challenges the idea underlying any such universal approach. He sees the world dividing into distinct civilisations, with the Chinese and Islamic civilisations disputing any claim of Western values to universality. If he is right then much of what is written above would be unrealistic nonsense. The UN would relapse into talkative impotence. Indeed Professor Huntington urges the West to look to its ramparts rather than suppose that it can contribute to a universal search for peace. If there are no shared values there can be no shared remedies.

There is a healthy warning here. The line of analysis in this book stretches from Vietnam to Versailles to Yalta and Potsdam to the UN in New York, that is from Europe across the Atlantic. History has given this background to today's international institutions. It cannot be guaranteed that the majority of nations who do not share that history will nevertheless accept its conclusions. We see, for example, disputes over the nature of human rights, ranging across a wide spectrum. At one edge Canadians and Scandinavians accept a generous interpretation of world-wide human rights as central to their foreign policy. At the opposite edge the Chinese subordinate political rights to mankind's need for a full belly. In the fast-growing environmental sector of international diplomacy a similar conflict is growing between the Western proposals for cleansing the planet by accepting restrictions on mankind's use of its resources, and the counter argument in developing countries that there must first be a fairer distribution of these resources.

These differences of background and of interest will continue, and may even intensify. The West has to curb a tendency to make patronising assumptions. Leaders of developing countries might in return restrain their tendency to mock and tease. For when every difference has been underlined there remain universal dangers which neither nation nor the groups that Professor Huntington calls 'civilisations' can cope with by themselves. Aggression, internal violence and organised crime are among the dangers common to us all.

As I worked on this book and the television series I was brought back again and again to the role of the United States – to a much greater extent than I expected when I began. The reason stands out clearly. In a world so constructed and so threatened we shall continue to need the leadership of the United States. The United States, for its part, will continue to need allies and international institutions. There will be material burdens to be shared in terms of money and occasionally of men and weapons. Congress and the American tax payer will not finance huge peacetime forces while their allies (and commercial competitors) do much less. There will be psychological burdens of decision taking that the United States will not wish to shoulder alone. After Vietnam the appetite for solitary adventure is not likely to return.

Of the allies, the most significant will be Europe and Japan. The institutional bickerings among European states about how they should work together on foreign policy make no sense to Americans. Henry Kissinger complained that there was no telephone number that he could ring to find out the views of Europe. We shall slowly and argumentatively move to provide his successors with that telephone number. This does not mean that they will always like what they hear when they ring up. On the contrary there will be occasions, for example in the Middle East, where a single European voice may declare a position different from that of the Americans. The two positions will then have to be reconciled if anything effective is to be done. What makes no sense is to suppose that in most of these questions there is value in a distinctive French, German or British voice. The problems of Cyprus, Turkey, the Baltic states require European participation if they are to be held in check, let alone solved.

The international institutions devised during the third phase of the search for peace are now being adapted to cope with the fourth. The changes in NATO have been well devised and so far been smoothly carried through. Here the type of continuous steady leadership practised by President Bush in the Gulf War is being continued in NATO matters by his successor. A steady policy has been explained to and accepted by Congress, the American public and the allies. With the United Nations the story has been sadly different. The Americans can reasonably complain that the UN has failed to adapt to the changed world and that it is water-logged with an excess of rival incoherent bureaucracies and extravagant rhetoric. Here the Administration has not so far managed to secure the consensus that is needed with Congress and the American public in favour of paying American dues in return for UN reform. It is in everyone's interest that this deal should be worked out and carried through as quickly as possible.

We have finally to return to the central theme of this book, namely the tension between realism and idealism which runs through all peace making. It is the main task of policy makers to reconcile the interests of nations and of communities within nations, rather than to further the spread of a particular set of ideas. It is not cynical to remark that interests rather than ideas govern most international decisions, for the clash of interests is usually less dangerous than the clash of ideas. But the ideas that blow across the world remain important in influencing how policy makers define their interests and the best ways of advancing them. The two dominant concepts of the moment are democracy and free trade and both are helpful in the search for peace.

Neither idea is all-conquering, but both have recently advanced far and fast. Who would have thought twenty years ago that Eastern Europe, Southern Africa and Latin America would by now be overwhelmingly composed of democracies? Who could have imagined NAFTA or felt sure that Europe would turn away from Fortress Europe and agree to whittle away the remnants of protectionism? These dominant ideas need not always or automatically serve the search for peace. A democracy can be fiercely nationalistic. It was not with the Greek colonels but with a democratic government that we had unreasonable trouble over Macedonia in 1993 and 1994. It has been argued that a democratic China might have more difficulty than did Chairman Mao in reining back nationalist feelings about Japan or Taiwan.

On the economic side free trade is certainly a cleansing wind but it can demolish frail structures on which poor people depend for shelter. Cash crops can distort a society. The main exception to Britain's advocacy of free trade has been our defence of some protection for vulnerable banana growers in the Windward Islands. I never felt ashamed in lining up on this in Europe with the French and Spaniards against our usual free trade allies. Doctrines carried to logical excess can provoke their opposites. But on balance the dominant winds at present blow favourably to peace.

But winds change. It is not difficult to foresee how free trade and deregulation could lose the intellectual and political support on which they now rest. New problems will certainly complicate future diplomacy in a way that would have amazed the statesmen at Vienna, Versailles, Yalta or Potsdam. As we have seen, national and international institutions will increasingly wrestle with the problems of the environment, climatic changes, drugs, population growth and migration, and pollution of all kinds. This set of anxieties may begin to pull the democratic world back towards restriction of trade and regulation of individual choice. Ordinary Americans may now feel more affected by drug-running and illegal immigration from Mexico than by any perceived threat from Russia. We are some way from the point where nations might use armed force to police recalcitrant polluters or others whose policies or lack of policy are so damaging that they could be held to constitute a sort of peaceful aggression. But it is perfectly possible to imagine economic sanctions and other techniques of pressure being wheeled forward in such cases.

Financial storms and earthquakes have seriously shaken the world in 1998. It is not certain whether the resulting fear will drive us together or further apart. Not before time Europe is worried about its competitiveness. Americans watch anxiously the growth of Chinese industry and become alarmed if a sinking Japanese yen intensifies the in-flow of Japanese products. Some of the shine has gone off NAFTA. Moreover these are early days for world free trade. We still believe in the West that we can survive growing competition while sustaining the costly welfare schemes that are characteristic of our own centrist politics, but not to be found among our Asian competitors. Our optimistic belief may be shaken as the competition intensifies. That would be the moment for the protectionists to become respectable. There is a little bit of protectionist in all of us. We in Europe and successive administrations have managed remarkably to keep it at bay in recent years. There is no Fortress Europe or Fortress North America. But the survival of open economic policies could be threatened by mounting unemployment or dropping living standards across the world.

I believe strongly in diplomacy. In the strained but by no means desperate world in which we live, the strains can be eased and collisions avoided by men and women who are ready to listen and allowed to compromise. As democracy strengthens across the world the policy makers have increasingly to carry public opinion with them. They will find themselves criticised by those in politics or the media who make their reputations or their fortunes out of tension and prejudice.

There is nothing wise or honourable in wearing jingoistic blinkers or trying to force such blinkers on others by frightening them with narrow prejudice. The bluster of xenophobia is a sign of weakness not of strength. But the policy maker has also to know the limits of idealism. What 'is' needs to be grasped and understood before he turns to what 'ought to be'. Leadership in the lay world is best exerted from a position of one step ahead of those who follow. The leader who in the search for glory places himself a hundred steps ahead of his electorate may feel magnificent until he finds that no one is following when he draws his sword.

We should not be impatient or dismayed by setbacks. This is a real difficulty for the idealist. You need the philosophical background of a Hammarskjöld to combine idealism with patience. The idealist tends to believe in a just and peaceful world as if it was a palace descended from heaven. He mourns over every broken pane and every room fouled by violence or hatred. He longs for the application of universal principles which could, he believes, make the palace whole and clean. The realist by contrast sees a building laboriously constructed from the ground upwards. He is not at all surprised that it takes a long time, or that occasionally bad weather undoes much of the work. He does not expect the design to be tidy or logical, or the outcome beautiful. He knows that the materials are defective, but they are the only ones available. He is surprised and pleased if people occasionally find that parts of the building offer real shelter. The danger for the realist is that he spends too much time leaning on his shovel or arguing about the measurements of a particular brick. The danger for the idealist is that discouragement leads to despair. Somewhere in the middle are those blessed with a mix of the two qualities. They are the ones who get something done.

Nothing ensures that we learn the lessons of history. We are perfectly capable of failing to stand on the shoulders of those who went before. Woodrow Wilson would have done better if he had studied the peace making of Vienna. Metternich might have found in the entrails of the dead French Revolution some doctrine of popular consent that could have preserved the Hapsburg dynasty. We are not automatically wiser than our predecessors. But I hope it is not the congenital optimism of the democratic politician that makes me reasonably optimistic about the fourth chapter of the search for peace.

We shall certainly experience setbacks and even disasters. But through study of past mistakes, through the careful balancing of interests, through the cautious harnessing of ideas, we have a reasonable prospect over the years of advancing three steps for every two we slide back.

INDEX

Warner Books now offers an exciting range of quality titles by both established and new authors. All of the books in this series are available from:

Little, Brown and Company (UK),
P.O. Box 11,
Falmouth,
Cornwall TR10 9EN.

Fax No: 01326 317444.
Telephone No: 01326 372400
E-mail: books@barni.avel.co.uk

Payments can be made as follows: cheque, postal order (payable to Little, Brown and Company) or by credit cards, Visa/Access. Do not send cash or currency. UK customers and B.F.P.O. please allow £1.00 for postage and packing for the first book, plus 50p for the second book, plus 30p for each additional book up to a maximum charge of £3.00 (7 books plus).

Overseas customers including Ireland, please allow £2.00 for the first book plus £1.00 for the second book, plus 50p for each additional book.

NAME (Block Letters) ....

....

ADDRESS ....

....

....

☐ I enclose my remittance for ....

☐ I wish to pay by Access/Visa Card

Number ☐☐☐☐☐☐☐☐☐☐☐☐☐☐☐☐

Card Expiry Date ☐☐☐☐